EESHA:

NO MORE SILENT TEARS

✻·✻·✻·✻·✻·✻·✻·✻·✻·✻·✻·✻·✻

breaking the silence of marital abuse

restoring hope

ELIZABETH KIRSTEN

Copyright © 2023 Elizabeth K. Steer

All rights reserved. No part of this publication may be reproduced, distributed, or transmitted in any form or by any means, including photocopying, recording, or other electronic or mechanical methods, without the prior written permission of the publisher, except in the case of brief quotations embodied in critical reviews and certain other noncommercial uses permitted by copyright law. For permission requests, please contact the author.

Scripture quotations are taken from the Holy Bible, New International Version ®, NIV ®, Copyright © 1973,1978, 1984, 2011 by Biblica Inc. ® Used by permission. All rights reserved worldwide.

Scripture quotations taken from the (NASB®) New American Standard Bible®, Copyright © 1960, 1971, 1977, 1995, 2020 by The Lockman Foundation. Used by permission. All rights reserved. Lockman.org

Scripture quotations taken from *The Holy Bible: The Amplified Bible*. 1987. 2015. La Habra, CA: The Lockman Foundation.

Scripture quotations taken from BSB The Holy Bible, Berean Standard Bible, BSB Copyright © 2016, 2020 by Bible Hub. All Rights Reserved Worldwide.

Scripture taken from the Good News Translation in Today's English Version- Second Edition Copyright © 1992 by American Bible Society. Used by Permission.

Scripture quotations marked TPT are from The Passion Translation®. Copyright © 2017, 2018, 2020 by Passion & Fire Ministries, Inc. Used by permission. All rights reserved. ThePassionTranslation.com.

Scripture taken from The Holy Bible: 21st Century King James Version (KJ21®) Copyright © 1994 by Deuel Enterprises, Inc. Gary, SD 57237, and used by permission.

The ESV Global Study Bible®, ESV® Bible Copyright © 2012 by Crossway. All rights reserved.

The Holy Bible, English Standard Version® (ESV®) Copyright © 2001 by Crossway, a publishing ministry of Good News Publishers. All rights reserved.

Some content taken from New Living Translation. Copyright © 1996. Used by permission of Tyndale House Publishers. All rights reserved.

Some content taken from the King James Bible which is ready for use as in the public domain.

Produced with the support of Tell Your Story Coaching

Dedication

This book is dedicated to Mary aka Daisy, my maternal grandmother who left an abusive spouse. This was around 1926, during a period in Jarrows' history of extreme poverty. She lived in a lodging house, in a single room with her young children, doing what had to be done to get enough food and rent, whilst caring for the bairns *(a Scottish term for children)*. There she met my Grandad, who as was the custom in those times, was also a drinker with violent outbursts. The wartime work on the ships and forays to the pub on the weekends kept him away often. I guess it was more tolerable because she stayed. He was apparently a very proud and educated man; kind in his way, and so not surprisingly living with someone else's children. Sometime later, now with two of his own born out of wedlock (one being my mum), his anger simmered just under the surface. He wouldn't commit bigamy yet had intimate relations leading to two children out of wedlock! He was not a man of faith, but a socialist, hating religion and all that it represented, "Hypocrites all of them," he would say concerning religious people. The irony is not wasted on me, I can assure you!

I also wish to dedicate this to all the women of faith, who steadfastly clung to the ashes of a once-roaring flame that led to a marriage covenant between themselves, their spouses, and God. The love of many really has grown cold, and though we can point to the wider population of the earth, none can see this more clearly than a woman unhappily trapped in a Christian marriage. The word of God, the Living Word has set you free, no longer are you in bondage to an unloving and therefore unbelieving spouse. The Law was put in place to demonstrate that mankind cannot ever live up to it unassisted by the spirit of God within them. You are free.

Endorsements

When I was studying to become a pastor, there was little training for how to help those who've suffered abuse. Imagine my surprise when I discovered it was a regular and common issue, I needed to help people escape and then recover from. Because of that, I'm so thankful Elizabeth has bravely written this book! It peels back the polished facade to reveal a rottenness underneath. Exposing such things is difficult to do well, but Elizabeth writes about these issues in a way that powerfully calls for action. Indeed, she shows that we have no alternative. All of us, especially within God's church, must learn to protect women in need, and more to the root, we must raise men from whom God's daughters need no rescue. Thank you, Elizabeth, for writing this much-needed book!

Nathanael White
Pastor and Leader
Presence Church, Minnesota, USA

This book blew my mind! Finally! A book that speaks into a very hidden but disastrously current reality of abuse for many people. Elizabeth writes from a place of love and her passion for justice is like a bright beam of hope that flows through the entire book. It's educational, informative, and insightful. Elizabeth knows the power of hope and freedom, not only because she has devoured and studied the Word of God which is weaved through this entire book, but also from her own experience of stepping out of oppressive, destructive marriages, and into the fullness that God offers. I'm excited for the many women who are trapped in abusive marriages, who will read this book and understand God's heart of love, peace, and hope for them. Freedom!

Jane Streatfield
Creator and Designer
"It's The Wonderful" Multi-Media Platform

Endorsements

This book blows the lid off of the seldom-discussed abuses that take place in marriages. Elizabeth carefully walks us through the common lies that are told and believed by Christians to hide the truth of destructive marital patterns. The book will not only bring these issues to light, but it also offers a solution and a path forward for those who have been harmed in these situations. The first step to solving any problem is acknowledging that there is one. This book will bring awareness to both those involved in the abusive situation as well as church leadership who are encouraged to handle these types of situations with the utmost care. This book will foster healing in the lives of many. I recommend this book to be read in church leadership circles and individual homes all over the world.

Daniella Ordonez
Story Creation Coach
Founder of Network for the Kingdom

Acknowledgements

I want first to thank Lin, who on a particular, you could say ordained day, had her listening ears on. Thank you for not judging me, and for you and your husband's wonderful support and belief in me. My heartfelt thanks to Daniella Ordonez, you have been a humble, firm, understanding and valuable book-writing coach, during an extremely challenging season in my life. You've helped and encouraged me in birthing this, the first of many books, my spiritual written offspring! Hopefully, her coaching and knowledge will be evidenced in these pages.

The passionate Kingdom mentor and leader, Pedro Adao, creator of the 100X Kingdom Entrepreneur Movement and Kingdom Seekers. Your "yes" gave room for my "yes!" I was kickstarted into momentum because of your faith and unrelenting pursuit of the Kingdom of God. You appeared on my radar by divine timing–a kairos moment. The Wisdom of the book of Proverbs, your 'hook', should be the mainstay of any believer. If Christ is our foundation, then surely, we can wholly depend upon wisdom, also known as lady wisdom or Holy Spirit. When humans walk in wisdom we exemplify the image of God, which is what we were created to do.

I would be remiss if I don't mention Jonathan Conrathe, an evangelist of excellence, a good shepherd walking in his Father's footsteps who preaches freedom to the captives. Your apostolic mentorship of our small house church in the nineties, and frank talks with me helped set me free! You showed me there was hope and freedom after abuse, and that divorce wasn't the end of the road as far as marriage was concerned. Freeing me from marriage to an unbeliever who feigned faith.

Also to Simon Gardner, for your prayers, and sound doctrinal and biblical beliefs. You stood by me, as a church leader in a climate in which that could be frowned on. Thank you both, I am now free to fly again! Last but not least, Prince Yinka Oyekan, for writing your book entitled *Manipulation, Domination and Control* way back in the day. Thank you for designing the School of Personal Transformation Course and taking it online! I learnt so much from your teaching, you both equipped and inspired me. My passion and yearning is to now model what you did, and in so doing lead others out of the wilderness.

The desert is such a barren place where the word is directed at you as a weapon to keep you from getting into a safe space or prevent you from placing safe boundaries, which when perceived like mirages disappear as the word becomes a weapon of destruction even in the mouth of a friendly Christian counsellor or your friend. The jungle where every offer of help or a listening ear, binds you ever tighter to a controlling oppressor, where you are cajoled and encouraged to do all in your power to save both the marriage and the spouse: to repress your feelings and needs, putting the needs of the husband first. A woman of virtue, who does all things, accepts all things, and gives you all things! That is not what this scripture means.

> *"And we know that in all things God works for the good of those who love him, who have been called according to his purpose." Romans 8:28, NIV*

Jesus was tested in the desert, in the wilderness he roamed, where the devil came and whispered carefully cherry-picked scripture, do you see that? Scripture is the very word of God. Tempting Jesus to throw himself over the cliff and past the boundary line. Encouraging Him to eat and drink from his table. Look at Job, his "wise" counsellors, who listened to the emotional tirades of Job, and then judged him after informing him it was his own sinfulness that was now falling on his own head! These tricks are still utilised every day in homes, to gain control and Lord it over the submissive woman. No more. It stops here. The start of the end of this hideous apostasy is upon us. This is "D-Day" and the victory belongs to the soldiers who advance and don't retreat.

In the words of a famous first lady of the UK, "You turn if you want to. The lady's not for turning!"

Preface

The purpose of this book is to reveal hidden abuse and oppression within Christian marriages. When your eyes are opened to this statistical reality, you will know you are not alone. There are shocking statistics that underpin this endemic evil which stalks behind closed doors. God and His word do not empower a man to dominate, but rather lead, by exemplifying the image of God as His image bearer. We must unfold the true sentiment behind the scripture Malachi 2:16, which is a verse often referred to in the conviction of women to stay unwaveringly obedient to a spouse and the Bible that has been perverted by human error and worldly influence. Revealing the truth behind this and other verses, which actually empower both victims and ministers of the true way alike, to seek the whole counsel of God in context.

I hope your greatest takeaway from this book is that the institution and covenant of marriage are not broken by a certificate of divorce, but rather by departure from the covenant. Departure manifested through the words, behaviours, and actions of an unsubmitted, unloving, misogynistic and/or legalistic husband towards his wife. If you are that woman, I hope it relieves you of the burden you've been carrying. This includes guilt, recrimination, doubts, hurts and anguish. If you are a friend, minister of religion, counsellor, or theologian, I hope you can see the truth of the love that Jesus, who is one with God, wants to be expressed towards His beloved image bearers–His bride/wife.

Preface i
What's The Big Idea? 1
My Story, His-Story 21
Eesha Or Ayzer 31
Disturbing And Acknowledging 39
Is It Abuse Or Oppression? 51
Did God Really Say? 59
Marriage And Divorce 71
Root Problem To Solution 81
Spiritual Abuse 95
Pornography 101
Coercion 109
Manipulation 117
Submit Or Retreat? 123
Signs Of Oppression/Abuse 139
Hide And Seek 147
Who Am I? 163
God's Favoured Women 171
Forgiveness 179
More Than A Conqueror 189
Contact The Author 195
Bibliography 197
References 199

Chapter One

What's The Big Idea?

The LORD God planted a garden toward the east, in Eden; and there He placed the man whom He had formed.
Genesis 2:8, NASB

Have you sometimes wondered what God had in mind when he put a man and a woman together? I mean, sometimes you just think, "How in the world was it ever supposed to work? We're so different, almost a different species!" There was that well-known book many years ago likening our differences in the same category to how different the planet Venus is from Mars! Well, there was more than a hint of observation in that I'd say! But God had a plan and a purpose to fulfil, right from the foundation of the earth. To populate the earth with godly offspring, born of His image, who themselves were made both male and female. I'll touch on this later on.

You Are Not Alone

In this book I hope to take you deeper into the underworld, behind closed doors, revealing to you that your circumstances are unfortunately not a rarity.

- 16 in 100 women are raped per year.
- 1/3, which is over 5 in 100, are raped in their own home.

- A recent study by Focus on the Family, which is a global Christian ministry, reports that sexual assault or forced sex occurs in 40-45% of marriage relationships.
- Marital rape occurs in 10-14% of all Christian marriages.

How do we reconcile this?

Jesus Christ only did what the Father did, He modelled marriage because He came to serve. God desired an intimate relationship with His created masterpieces. In the garden known as Eden, He walked and talked with them in the cool of the day. Until one day, they chose another father figure known as the father of lies. God then reinstated the relationship, starting with Father Abraham. Centuries later, Jesus, the second Adam but God's first begotten son, our saviour, brought us freedom! I'll say it again, because it's worth repeating, He brings freedom. To the captive, He is a bondage breaker. He breaks chains! You don't lose your personal freedom by repressing your desires, needs, and feelings when you enter into a marriage covenant.

I would suggest there are at least four reasons you should finish this book:

1. You've suffered abuse and it's taken you years to realise that's what it is. If you have not recognized it, then perhaps a good friend has told you that what's happening to you is abuse.
2. You've felt at times that your marriage may be abusive but rationalise it as really only a blip. You say things like, "It's not like he's hitting me all the time, and if I go along with his desires and sacrifice my own it'll get better."
3. You know for certain that your marriage is abusive, yet feel separation or divorce is unbiblical. As a couple or at least one of you is in ministry, or high-profile church leadership, there is a lot at stake.

4. You know someone who has suffered neglect and abuse or has told you they have, and perhaps you've doubted them.

Influenced by Christianity and Buddhism, Bell Hooks who identifies as queer, writes in her book *All About Love: New Visions*: "All too often women believe it is a sign of commitment, an expression of love, to endure unkindness or cruelty, to forgive and forget. In actuality, when we love rightly, we know that the healthy, loving response to cruelty and abuse is putting ourselves out of harm's way."

If that doesn't convince you, then read the statistics:
- Domestic abuse will affect one in four women and one in six men in their lifetime.
- It leads to, on average, two women being murdered each week and thirty men per year. Rape accounts for sixteen percent of all violent crimes. Violent crime is the least likely to be reported to the police.
- Has more repeat victims than any other crime. On average, there will have been thirty-five assaults before a victim calls the police.
- It is the single most quoted reason for becoming homeless.
- In 2010, the Forced Marriage Unit responded to one thousand seven hundred and thirty-five reports of possible forced marriages.
- In addition, approximately four hundred people commit suicide each year who have attended the hospital for domestic abuse injuries in the previous six months. Two hundred of these attend hospital on the day they go on to commit suicide.
- Only one in one hundred rapes were recorded by police in 2021.

- The year ending March 2022 saw the highest-ever recorded rape figures, out of 70,330 charges only 2,223 were brought in. 1 in 2 were against women
- Ninety-eight percent of adults prosecuted for rape are men.
- Five in six rapes against women are carried out by someone they know. Additionally, five out of six don't report it. Forty percent because of embarrassment, thirty-eight percent because they thought the police couldn't help, and thirty-four percent because it would be humiliating.
- Six hundred and eighteen thousand women are raped or sexually assaulted each year. That's one in thirty-five women. At least one woman you know was likely raped or sexually assaulted in the last year.
- One in three survivors of rape experience it in their home.

NOTE: See Reference page at the back of the book for resources and more information.

Domestic violence is prevalent within the United Kingdom Church community, with almost one-fifth or nineteen percent of adults having experienced their partner refusing to accept no for an answer when he or she wants to have sex. According to an exclusive survey conducted by *Premier Christianity Magazine,* six percent of the four hundred forty-three people who completed the survey, which was held in conjunction with domestic abuse charity titled, Restored, as part of their "In Churches Too" campaign, this is a frequent experience.

In an article by Darby Strickland, the Focus on the Family writer reports that sexual assault or forced sex occurs in forty to forty-five percent of marriage relationships, and marital rape occurs in ten to fourteen percent of all marriages. Additionally, the annual divorce rate among married women with a non-religious upbringing is around five percent. For religious women, it's around 4.5

percent. For balance and reflection, I've included some figures for sex trafficking in 2021 and 2022. The figures I've collated are from information on the *unseenuk.org* website.

Please note, I am not equating domestic violence with sex trafficking here. What I'm trying to say is that percentage-wise, the crime of domestic violence is more prolific than human trafficking, which does get brought to peoples' attention. Yet within the context of the church, marital abuse is not addressed. Whilst victims of domestic abuse and oppression could find relief, escape, and support more readily than victims of trafficking, their plight is rarely recognised nor handled with care. The married oppressed are usually lured and tricked, whilst those caught up in human trafficking are lured, tricked, but also drugged or bought. They most often have multiple abusers as well. There is public awareness of human trafficking, and charities to support. There is also a general awareness and support for people, mostly women and children, suffering abuse within society at large. Yet apparently, no one who is part of a church or faith group suffers from this, much fewer need support and shelter. Human trafficking is fuel for the porn industry, which often leads men to sexual abuse or labour for trading between cartels, influencers, and millionaires who care little about the suffering of those they enslave for their amusement and self-gratification. Remember ninety-eight percent of all rape is carried out by males. I can't call them men or animals as that would be an insult to good men and the animal kingdom.

Worldwide one in two hundred people are enslaved and trafficked. Seventy-one percent are women and girls. A slave is forced to work against their will, owned or controlled by their exploiter, and has limited freedom of movement. More than 50% of those in forced labour are doing so under threat, intimidation, or coercion.

United Kingdom Sex trafficking victims accounted for 1 in 4 of 1% of the population in 2021. Figures rose in 2022. It still remained as a quarter of a percent of the population. That's 1 in 400. Yet 12 in 400 women are raped per year. That's three times more. 4 in 400 in their own home (3% and 1% from the figure 1 in 35 women in the statistics mentioned on pages 3 – 4).

Women who are suffering physical, sexual, financial, emotional, mental, and spiritual oppression including rape in their own homes, are extremely likely to be living in conditions where they have unwittingly become slaves to a domineering and controlling man. The money is controlled and supervised by the exploiter, and many are forced to work both at home and in the workplace. Many are controlled by their exploiter, having limited freedom of movement, being denied access to friends and family, and having sole responsibility for looking after children, home, and spouse. They have their conversations, movements, and social interactions monitored. They may also be expected to perform sexual duties and perversions on demand or be in a position where an adulterous and promiscuous situation occurs. All of this is in silence. They hide bruises, both physical and invisible. Just for clarity, pornography is adultery against God and the spouse. Nonconsensual sex and penetration in marriage is rape. God does not condone rape. Just because it's in the Bible, and God doesn't cause it to cease, doesn't make it right. Remember, God didn't desire the blood of animal sacrifices, yet it's in the Bible, and they still did it:

> For it is impossible for the blood of bulls and goats to take away sins. Therefore, when He comes into the world, He says, "You have not desired sacrifice and offering, but you have prepared a body for me; You have not taken pleasure in whole burnt offerings and offerings for sin." Then I said, "Behold, I have come (it is written of me in the scroll of the book) to do your will, O God" (Hebrews 10:4-7, NASB).

What's The Big Idea?

In a church that has fifty women, there could be at least three women who are experiencing or have experienced sexual abuse or have suffered marital rape, and also two divorced women. Let me just state that I acknowledge men get abused, and I know five men who have suffered historical sexual abuse by males, however, I've only met one man who was abused by his wife in all my life. I know many women, myself included, who have been at worst shunned, and at best mistrusted and overlooked when it comes to membership and serving (front of house serving), because of separation from spouse or getting divorced. Considering they are already facing personal crisis', this is alarming enough, but to think that there could be a hidden history of abuse in this woman's life makes this a further case of spiritual, mental, and emotional abuse, which reaffirms to the woman that she is rejected and soiled. Not a good example to set. Jesus allowed the woman with the alabaster jar to minister front of house!

Marriage, in the Bible, is said to be a symbol of Jesus's sacrificial love, a sacrifice from the husband Jesus. His wife is the church, His pure and spotless bride. In the word, it says, "I have loved you with an everlasting love, therefore I have loved you with everlasting devotion" (Jeremiah 31:3, BSB) The Hebrew word used for devotion here is chêsêd which means goodness and kindness. God here was talking to Israel, with whom He'd made a marriage type of covenant.

When is it abuse, and when is it not? Is this oppression? Well, that depends on many complex contributing factors. Below I give a real-life example. Some of these things, as a stand-alone occurrence, are fairly innocuous, but as a whole, they paint a different picture, and I think you'll agree.

OVERLOOKED OR REJECTED?

Tina had started attending a new church, one her husband didn't attend. They had been in separate rooms for six months already. He had been dealing with an online porn addiction for forty years, including ten years of their marriage, and despite seeking help each time, she caught him still engaging in sexual activity with online women. They were essentially separated, as divorce was not an option. When she approached her church leader, she told him outright that she was no longer submitting to her husband, due to his unbelief born out of his actions. She agreed to submit to his leadership when in his church, and church activities. After some time, she offered her support within the church in whatever activity would help. Tina became the cleaner and went in twice a week before or after work to clean. Eventually, she was unable to do this anymore due to additional commitments during the hours the church was unlocked but not in use. She was never asked to assist or support in any other way, despite offering and having been in church leadership and on the worship team for many years before attending this church. Eventually, Tina was accepted on a team in a supporting role. It was evident to her that only married couples managed to be in supporting and ministry roles. Tina eventually let her attendance levels slip. She was made for so much more than this. Being pew fodder was not for her. Due to her circumstances at home, she had lost some of her confidence, so she didn't approach the leadership again. Though she had, in varying degrees, let them know of her previous ministry roles.

Now a friend of hers, an accomplished musician, was told directly that until she and her partner of over eight years, who had become a believer, got married, she wouldn't be able to serve 'front of house'. This is despite her partner moving out of their home to allow his partner to be fulfilled in her role until they were married.

I aim to help you find your voice, by initially being a voice for you, encouraging you to be bold and unashamed of your past, or present circumstances. We can only help reduce this atrocity if we enter into a healthy dialogue. This oppression has to stop, but first,

What's The Big Idea?

it needs to be acknowledged and recognised. How can the church at large begin to tackle this insidious endemic if victims remain silent? The main problem is that many women will remain silent, even if prompted or given an opportunity. The question then is why, and how do we create an environment that allows dialogue? A safe, loving, and compassionate dialogue with individuals will only happen when we learn to read God's word correctly and listen to wounded women unbiasedly. Some women may never feel safe enough to speak. Some may not have the freedom to speak. Some may feel that if they do, they will have to face a backlash from an affronted spouse who sees no error. In these cases, if we suspect something, then we must remain vigilant, keep them engaged with genuine friendship, and be ready to ask the right questions at the right time. There are many books, forums, blogs, and support groups that can be searched out on the internet. I have found so many when researching for personal support and then for this book.

If you are married and unhappy, or someone you know is, some problems need addressing, not least the possible absence of an opportunity for being heard. Things need to change, and I'll be as bold as to suggest that it might be you that needs to change first. Which is precisely what you or someone who's talked to you has been told. For it is more often the women who are usually the ones seeking counsel, and this is what we hear most of the time! Bear with me a while, though that may bring up strong feelings, I am for you not against you. Prepare to have your eyes opened, and your senses restored. It's time to about turn! It's high time we changed our minds!

It's our mind that needs to change because the mind is the main battleground. And here, on this battlefield is where there are far too many casualties and corpses. I believe that some guided Bible scriptures will reveal the solution to this silence-inducing tragedy that is hidden behind the walls and doors of homes and churches. Before you go on, grab a notebook, a Bible, or better still a few if you have them, and refer to them so you can see for yourself the words that differ from Bible to Bible, and from one era to another. You can also get some useful online Bible apps, where you have a choice of versions at your fingertips. I have provided the scriptures here, but don't just take my word for it, too many of us have done that for way too long. Remember, if someone quotes 'the word' at you to keep you trapped, that is witchcraft. It was Satan's strategy to enslave Yeshua, our Jesus. And if someone says you are not using an accurate translation, point them to the plethora of available ones, including very accurate Hebrew and Aramaic translations. Then leave them to it. If they have to fight you with the word, it shows they are fighting you.

"It's the goodness of God that leads us to repentance" (Romans 2:4, NIV). The Greek word here for repentance is metanoia, which means "changing one's mind," it is commonly understood as "a transformative change of heart". When we change our minds, our actions then need to line up with that change. Then our heart starts being transformed as we lean into grace. I am speaking to victims here and am not referring to the commonly accepted version of that word being directed at someone who has sinned, but rather to someone who has had sin committed against them!

> "Do not conform to the pattern of this world but be transformed by the renewing of your mind. Then you will be able to test and approve what God's will is—his good, pleasing, and perfect will" (Romans 12:2, NIV).

When I think back to the day I spilt out to Lin what was going on within my marriage, I can now laugh! She was gobsmacked, angry, disgusted, and indignant on my behalf, all at the same time! Almost apoplectic! From then on, she pursued me and my welfare, it became one of her mandates, she would not let go until I relented, opening my eyes to the absurdity of my circumstances.

What's The Big Idea?

But at the time, sad to say, though I knew things weren't right, I just had come to a place where I wouldn't rock the boat. My spouse and I had drawn up our battle lines and then retreated to the trenches. There seemed to be no way through. By degrees, our marriage had eroded to being a marriage of inconvenience. All but two children had flown the nest, some having relationship issues. The two at home? One, an adult, resorted to a near monastic existence retreating into drugs and gaming. Having had three broken relationships, he seemed to simply give up. The other was disabled, and that's a whole nother story. Both of these children indirectly worsened the situation, and initially being a blended family of seven, things often came to a head, forcing personal challenges into the recesses.

Children of these types of homes, where actions (and inactions) speak louder than words, often grow up with a warped view of faith, respect, and marriage. It's no wonder they often leave the faith and go on to perpetuate a fallen, disparate paradigm of intimate relationships that were meant to reproduce godly offspring. Like a wounded animal, I had retreated into the back of the cage. And like any wounded animal, I refused to let any others see that I was suffering and broken. Oh no! That would dishonour God, who would never leave me in a pit of despair. I was made to carry God's glory, a glory carrier, proclaiming the good news of redemption through access to His Kingdom promises in the here and now. I thought I knew for certain what blind faith meant, that's for sure. I could live with the internal pain, but I could not let God down. Oh, the pride displayed by that sentiment. Well, my friend certainly helped me to change my mind, it was up for renewal anyway. So, I upgraded and installed the latest version and read The Word through a different lens!

One of my goals within these pages is to reveal the true meanings of words, context, and etymology (which is the evolution of a word from its first use to its present use). Our words are often thought of as weapons, and the sharpest of weapons is God's word. Weapons can tear down and build up. Oftentimes a woman married to an oppressor has been torn to shreds by words alone. Her spirit was broken, and her identity shattered into a million pieces. Hurting and deserted by those around her who know little of what is said and done to her. They, and you, could not begin to imagine or empathise unless you've experienced it yourselves.

The Bible is a weapon that is supposed to protect you, but it can become a weapon turned against you. That double-edged sword can perform surgery, but it can pierce through a victim just as much as it does the devil's heart. In the wrong hands, it can be fatal, sealing the doom of many who revere the words within almost as much as the Lord God Himself. Many people groups for centuries have been enslaved, oppressed, and imprisoned by the words within, all in the name of God through religion. And before the written word, the oral tradition was used similarly. The Bible has always caused division both amongst followers of Christ, people who believe in God, and between faith groups and secular society.

Here I'm taking a closer look at the plight of Christian women, who either refuse to leave an abuser-oppressor or are entreated to stay in marriages where a husband is maintaining power, in the name of Godly authority, to the point of abuse-oppression. Within its hallowed pages, we will search out the true meaning, context and intent of those words which are so often used to maintain power over a weaker subject. The written word of God, known as the Bible, is a collection of accounts, poetry, books of wisdom, letters, and written history. Some from handed down oral history, hieroglyphics and cuneiform which is so-called because of the shape of a cut-off reed pressed into clay. There are king lists and genealogies, which people of God were inspired to write. Others continued copying it over the centuries, and inevitably some errors

What's The Big Idea?

were made. To dogmatically insist on the contrary to defend God, is errant at best. God defends Himself. As linguists, historians, and archaeologists combine with anthropologists, ancient texts including scripture can be better understood, especially when light is shone onto parts that don't make sense. Context, colloquialisms, and cultural nuances can change things quite a bit. The more we know, the more is revealed. I believe that what Jesus told us about most was the Kingdom, not the church. Kingdom is His domain, His homeland, and ours too when we follow Him into it. That is why we were told in Genesis, to take dominion of the earth. As in Heaven, so on earth! The church is His bride, the kingdom is His domain!

We are the church bride. As a body, we are supposed to be encouraging one another. So we attain the full realisation of our authority and freedom. We realise how worthy and valued we are, a bride spotless, not because of cleaning ourselves up, but because He's already done it! However, we also have a duty of obedience to honour what He's done. When church becomes a thing we do, not something we are, we lose genuine relationships with each other. Yes, gather together, but if we do, let's get to know one another properly. We should preach by our actions, all of us, not just a preacher at the front. Yes, they have been led to scripture that perhaps God has laid on them, to reveal a truth, to impart wisdom. But we are all priests and kings. We all have knowledge, wisdom, and inspiration, and we have all discovered truths and nuggets to share. Don't just leave it to a ministry team to seek out the lost, lonely, confused, or hurt. Are there people at your place of gathering that always seem quiet, or disappear very quickly once the main service ends? Have you ever talked to a woman who has suggested there is abuse at home? What about a man who seems to go on about the wife, even jokingly? Have you got to know others well enough that this would even come up?

My immediate response? This is an issue that we need to talk about. In Christian society, we have talked about porn, poverty, Black Lives Matter, addiction, human trafficking, and child abuse, just to name a few; but where is the acknowledgment of this silent assassin? How are we to bring correct biblical living into our lives as an example and witness to those around us if we're not even aware there's a problem?

Another thing I'd like to point out is that not only are there born-again believers suffering, but within a healthy thriving church community, we will meet many seekers and new believers who may be experiencing domestic abuse or domestic physical violence. How do we counsel them? If they are walking with the Lord now, but their unbelieving spouse or partner is not? The purpose of this book is to reveal to you that marital oppression of Christian women is a very real problem. One that isn't talked about much, if at all, in religious circles. I hope to reveal both the problem and solution right under our noses! Not only are Christian women being used, but they are being misused and abused.

Secondly, I wish to show you how the Bible, which has at times been utilised as a strong tool and motivator for dealing with problems we may face, has been improperly used, misread, and at times mistranslated. Particularly where divorce and how to deal with conflict is concerned. "All Scripture is breathed out by God and profitable for teaching, for reproof, for correction, and for training in righteousness" (2 Timothy 3:16, ESV).

Thirdly, I want you to fully comprehend just how much God loves you. To know how worthy you are, and how marriage is not the place for having to be long-suffering and dealing with pain inflicted by the spouse. Forgiveness doesn't mean allowing it to continue, nor having to live with ill-treatment, bullying, and all other kinds of oppression. God hates abuse. Divorce doesn't end the marriage, a man who is breaking a covenant with God and his wife

What's The Big Idea?

does! "You shall love the Lord your God with all your heart, and with all your soul, and with all your strength, and with all your mind, and your neighbour as yourself" (Luke 10:27, ESV).

The Bible tells us we should,

> "learn to do good; seek justice, and correct oppression" (Isaiah 1:17, ESV).

Was I doing this? Well, I wasn't correcting oppression then, but I intend to now! And are you loving others as yourself? I confess, at times I don't. Even now, after all this time, and also in writing this, I am still saddened by my steadfast naivety. I am so glad that the Lord saved me from myself, and the oppressive environment, which I might add, was exacerbated by a plethora of other issues throughout our marriage: two rounds of cancer, a disabled child, aging/dying parents respectively, and the misdemeanours of and altercations with our blended family. My friends and my church leader led me through the word of God and supported me in whatever decision I chose to make. I decided to leave first, to sort out my wounds and get my heart healed, and then only after that did I expend energy on seeking a divorce. My freedom had just started, I was out of the cage, but had gotten so accustomed to those confines, that it took a while to spread my wings and fly again.

This book is very needed here and now. When I was still trapped, there was so very little information for believers. Sure, secular society had begun taking this seriously, with help offered in many areas. However, our Christian worldview is very different, after all, we're accountable to the church, and to God Himself. This is also evidenced by the rose-tinted glasses with which we view our institutions such as a church, marriage, and work for instance.

We've seen the alarming statistics collated by some Christian organisations already. I share some of my story, and briefly that of others I've known. This book will at times be frank, injected with humour, as I've discovered in my journey, this helps soften the blow to the senses. If you are still residing with an oppressor and/or have children who can read, I'd advise caution on leaving it lying around. If there's a chance of violence, seek help in constructing a safe exit plan.

In revealing the whole concept of marriage, I briefly review the history of God's people and His desire to enter into a covenant relationship with them, which will ultimately be fulfilled through the return of the resurrected Christ to claim His bride (wife). I explain a misnomer that we are just Ezers, or 'helpers' demonstrating how scripture can and has been used to entrap humans for millennia.

We can only solve a problem when it's been identified. We can only see a thing when we look at the bigger picture. This book will show you the bigger picture, and then zoom in on the immediate problem. We must treat this as a very real and pressing issue because that is what it is. The book aims to bring the darkness into the light, revealing this silent assassin, creating awareness, empathy, and a platform for dialogue, dispelling the myth surrounding a misquote of a certain scripture regarding divorce! Specifically, "For I hate divorce, says the LORD the God of Israel" (Malachi 2:16, AMP). It should read like this,

"For the Lord, the God of Israel, saith that He hateth (is an enemy of) putting away (forsaking): for one covereth (conceals/hides) violence (cruelty, injustice) with his garment (his wife) saith the Lord of hosts: therefore take heed to your spirit that you deal not treacherously" (Malachi 2:16, KJV).

God may well dislike divorce or separation, but who doesn't? Especially when it's because a man has finished with or no longer loves his wife. What this scripture is pointing out is that God hates violence (treachery) towards a wife, not just the divorce itself.

We'll journey together from the inception of the human race to the present day. From not knowing to "Houston, we have a problem!"

What's The Big Idea?

Learning there is a problem is good, but actively dealing with it is another matter entirely. So I also make suggestions on how to identify, and approach this issue. By the end, I hope you will be resolved to ending at least the hiddenness, and possibly become a friend or confidante who can confidently support a woman with issues. WWJD is an acronym that stands for, *What Would Jesus Do*? What did Jesus say to the woman with the issue of blood? "Daughter, be of good comfort, your faith (evidenced by counter-cultural action) has made you saved, delivered, and protected." Made whole, the word is sozo, pronounced sode-zo. It's the same word as salvation! Note, He immediately referred to her as family when He said "daughter!"

> "The Spirit of the Lord is upon me because he has anointed me to proclaim good news to the poor. He has sent me to proclaim liberty to the captives and recovering of sight to the blind, to set at liberty those who are oppressed, to proclaim the year of the Lord's favour"
> (Luke 4:18-19, ESV).

I am anointed to proclaim the good news! Are you crushed and poor in spirit? I'll set you free from captivity and open your eyes to the scriptures. Say goodbye to oppression as the favour of the Lord was yours the day Jesus rose to new life! You are His beloved, not another person's punching bag, servant, slave, or prostitute. We are a servant of His firstly and not man first because all that we do in Kingdom life is as if it's for Him. He doesn't expect you to serve an ungodly husband. Win him over, by all means, but not by doing whatever he expects, asks, or demands. He says, if you do try to win him over and still he stays unchanged, you are free to leave. There is no covenant between an unbelieving husband and a believing wife! If he treats you in a way he wouldn't treat Jesus, He is not a believer. If he takes part in things that are against the law of love, again if Jesus was there, he wouldn't do it, then he's not a believer! His behaviour is a manifestation of his attitude toward God. The way he is towards you is the way he is toward God. It is no longer you who lives in that body but the spirit of God. Jesus said, what you do to these little ones, is what you do to me. We are His children. You are His child!

By the time you've reached the end of this book, I promise you will know God loves you and that divorce is not a sin. You will know your identity, because I'm going to affirm and reaffirm, through scripture that you are worthy, loved, and treasured. You will also be equipped to assist others in transitioning into their identity. Your identity was sealed in Christ the day you first believed.

> "The ultimate tragedy is not the oppression and cruelty by the bad people, but the silence over it by the good people."
> – Martin Luther King Jr. (From a speech given in 1965)

PRAYER

Lord, please forgive me for looking the other way. When I didn't do it for the least of these, I didn't do it for you. Sorry that I've been a stumbling block and a hindrance to your redemptive plan. Please forgive me.

Please know Lord, that I acknowledge that I shrunk back, for fear of man, from doing the right thing. For not confronting sin, and instead allowing it.

Lord, please lead me to those who are lost, not just those of no faith, but also to those of faith who have lost their way. Help me to proclaim freedom to the captive. And Lord, let me be captivated by your love for me, so I can manifest that love outwards and wear it as a garment of praise. In Jesus, Yeshua Ha Mashiac's name. Amen.

Chapter Two

My Story, His-Story

"How precious it is, Lord, to realize you are thinking about me constantly! I can't even count how many times a day your thoughts turn towards me"
(Psalm 139:17, TLB)

The reasons for this book are many, but right up there is that for more than twenty-eight years I have experienced abuse during two marriages. One to a believer in God who talked the talk. The other to a follower of Jesus Christ walking the walk. Believe me, the difference is relevant here. In the first instance, there is no pretense of submission to God's appointed and anointed King! The devil believed in God, and he was conversant in the scriptures too! But Satan was not submitted to God, nor Christ. In short, if your spouse is doing unbiblical deeds, he fits into the first category, or talking the talk.

The abuse ranged from the typical obvious and recognisable physical and sexual abuse to the more subtle, insidious, sometimes baffling, and confusing dialogue and actions in the day-to-day and nightly course of married life. Such as selfishness, constant tracking of my movements and whereabouts, temper tantrums or sulking (both are manipulation), confusion (gaslighting), coercion (manipulation again), inflicting pain (emotionally and/or sexually), and control or dominating behaviour. There was also sexual degradation, adultery, pornography (which is sexual adultery through masturbation with women in still images, moving images, or via phone calls), and coerced or forced and/or painful sex.

It can appear on their part, either unrecognized/subconscious (demonic) or recognised/intentional (self-centred also known as narcissistic or power hungry). Sometimes there's the blame game or excuses. They say things like, "'If you would only…" or "I can't help it, it's an addiction" or "I had a poor father or no father as a role model." They might also say, "It's you because you didn't have a proper father figure" or "It's your mother's fault." What is the cherry on the cake? You may hear, "'I'm so sorry, I won't do it again," usually with the addition of, "In the Bible, it says to forgive seventy times seven times or "You have to be nice to me if you've truly forgiven!"

If it's a repeated occurrence, and it causes you anxiety, fear, disgust, pain, or a belief that you are like a child who needs to be told what you can and cannot do, it's abuse. If your free will or desires are being overridden, it's abuse. An abuse of authority. An abdication of responsibility, in both senses of the words bad husbandry! Collins dictionary synonyms of the noun husbandry, "thrift (being careful or caring), economy (good stewardship), good housekeeping (keeping it all in good order), frugality (not overzealous with finances), careful management (self-explanatory).

"From inside, a fish can't see that it's in a bowl." - Elizabeth Kirsten

<u>Let me introduce myself, in brief, here is some of my story:</u>
In 1989, at the age of twenty-nine, I began to see a man who was separated from his wife. His children were living with him, he had a good work ethic, and their home was a clean and tidy welcoming environment with pets, a garden, and a garage. In short, it was just the stability I needed at that stage in my life. I moved in fairly quickly and by 1992, we were married and had a 9-month-old little boy!

By 2002, we had three children of our own and two from his first wife on weekends. I was not ok. The damage of years of

My Story, His-Story

bullying via mental, physical, and sexual abuse, his initial affair with a good friend of mine, followed by his relationship with an air hostess, finally took its toll. I was a shadow of my former self. I'd had to flee from the home with all three of our children a couple of times under threatening conditions and was terrified of making him angry. Leaving him wasn't going to be a walk in the park. I had come to Christ in 1994 (two years after we married) and had a close community of faith-filled friends, but they couldn't protect me in my own home. Ultimately, he left, but it was far from over.

In 2000, we'd taken in a lodger, who was a believer. Initially, I was reticent, but my husband insisted. He was still in situ when my husband left in 2002, and as my husband had stopped paying all bills, it was money I needed. At least until I could find a job that suited school times. The lodger and I got on well and had friends in common. On Sundays, after church, I'd often have them come to mine and we'd have a shared lunch and an afternoon of shared spontaneous worship and fellowship. It meant I kept all the excess food, which was great, as I was by now in need of it! Other friends delivered food parcels anonymously. This man and I, at some point, acknowledged there was a spark of something more than fondness between us. I should have known better.

One terrible night, after a fun evening together things got out of hand very quickly, and he forced himself on me. I fled to my friend's house, and she witnessed the bruises on the top of the inner part of my thighs. I didn't press charges, and he left. In 2003, I moved away to the coast with my children. I needed a new life. Two of my friends drove a hired Luton van full of my household goods to our newly rented home. Three months later I paid cash for a new house and the children and I moved in just before Christmas. One of the friends came back to visit just two months later.

So started a new relationship, slowly at first as I was quite hesitant. Eventually, I was all in. As I reflect, I could see so many disturbing warning signs, not least that he had been persistent and resolute on entering into an intimate relationship, whilst I insisted, rather weakly ultimately, on staying pure until we got married. I wanted to have a period of purification, a little Esther-like after my previous sexual encounters. He was a spirit-filled spirit believer, romantic, and generous (yes, I had blinkers on). He still lived nearly two hundred miles away, as he felt it wrong to move in. The truth was probably that he wanted things to appear above board to the outside world.

He pushed past my feeble boundaries time and time again. Why do I say feeble boundaries? It is because I hadn't built up a boundary before embarking on another relationship. I was supposed to be finding myself after the previous two seasons, and refreshing myself emotionally, mentally, and spiritually. The little foxes come to mind in Song of Solomon 2:15, "Catch the foxes for us, The little foxes that are ruining the vineyards, While our vineyards are in blossom." Though I had grown to love him, in part I felt I had to marry him so the consequences of God's immutable laws would be mitigated.

Little did I know what lay ahead. I had been playing with fire and was about to get burnt. The lesson here, retrospectively, is that it's better to confess a deep error and repent before God, than to literally in this case, get into bed with a narcissistic oppressor and repent at leisure. The trap the enemy had set for me was so subtle, I didn't see it coming, even though I had already developed a sense that this man had low moral principles and an inflated sense of confessed brilliance/superiority. I guess I felt, because of my compliance-consent, that I too had a moral compass that had gone adrift, and so chose to drift around in a compass-less wilderness where I lost all sense of direction for a long while. Well, I guess I found myself! I found myself in a whole big mess, that's for sure. One that ultimately presented the very option I had bypassed, to place myself in the arms of a loving Father and learn how to be loved. But it was not without extreme cost.

By 2006, we'd got married and our honeymoon baby, a life-threatened complex disabled child had been born. Life had taken us by storm. Like being hit by a high-speed train. To me, it felt a bit like the biblical rendition of Bathsheba and David. Our world was tipped upside down. I felt that God had deserted me. But the truth was, I was simply lost.

What followed was years and years of constant high-octane stress, grief, and situations spiraling out of control. The children rebelled and got into all sorts of scrapes. Our disabled son had frequent appointments, hospital admissions, and near-death situations. We had many strangers in our house for appointments, home visits, and carers. All of this was compounded by my husband's now apparent insecurity, hurtful accusations, lying, his not-very-well-hidden addiction to pornography, his refusal to contribute to the household running costs, and his complete reliance on me for everything. In short, not carrying any responsibility.

Ultimately, though, the final nail in the coffin was the sexual perversions in our bed including fellatio and anal penetrative sex. All this as well as his insistence that I perform my marital sexual duties as the Bible says, despite our constant crisis state, my menopause, a mental health crisis, and two long periods of breast cancer. I'd had enough. In April 2021, after three years in a separate bedroom, I left my home, possessions, child, pets, and old dead life. My grown-up children had long fled the nest, his grown-up son by his previous marriage still installed, ruling the roost with his addictions, and temper outbursts. Our disabled child, a 14-year-old, was the equivalent of a baby needing twenty-four-seven care, so I was in my former home almost daily to care for him. Just a few months ago, aged sixteen and three-quarters, he passed into glory after a short mild illness. I was in the process of dealing with round three of breast cancer following a single mastectomy and ongoing treatment. The divorce and settlement are still in process. Life hasn't gotten any easier, though I really do hope and indeed trust that the worst is behind me.

This is my story. It required boldness on my part, and ears to hear. The past is behind me, my present is here, and I intend to take captivity captive, and release others through and for the joy that is set before me. Today I choose to bless.

Life, fairly often, isn't easy for a follower of Christ, and at times, the battles can overwhelm us. But we have an advocate in heavenly places. He lifts our arms for battle and is the lifter of our heads! He loves us with everlasting love. His purpose for us is to have life in abundance. I still believe that despite everything. I want to entreat you to enter into a journey with me. A journey through the Bible with a humble heart. A journey to renew your mind, so that you may come to a place of renewed strength; so that you may be able to hold up the arms of abuse victims, and if you are, or feel you may be a victim, you will have your strength renewed, and fly like an eagle.

> "Now the Lord is the Spirit, and where the Spirit of the Lord is, there is liberty [emancipation from bondage, true freedom]. And we all, with unveiled face, continually seeing as in a mirror the glory of the Lord, are progressively being transformed into His image from [one degree of] glory to [even more] glory, which comes from the Lord, [who is] the Spirit" (2 Corinthians 3:17-18, AMP).

Let God minister His word to you, throughout this book. Cross-reference the scriptures I share. Look at other translations. Listen to the Spirit of God. Trust the process. Trust me, I didn't go through all I've experienced for nothing. I refuse to sit in a dark cave licking my victim wounds, whilst others are needing to be free. I am a thriver, not just a survivor. If you absorb what is written here and, in the Bible, you will be a thriver too, I promise. My name means promise or oath of God! That is why covenants are so important to me. A covenant is a promise, written as a legally binding contract that is ratified by a legal process and/or royal assent. Covenants are important to God because embedded in them are His promises.

THEIR STORIES

In these pages, there will be real-life situations, accounts, and statistics from many traceable and respected sources. I show how Bible texts differ from the original, and how scriptures are quoted out of context, and/or from translations that don't match with the original words of scripture. Speaking biblical words over a wife that is deemed errant, is utilized by husbands and other Christians to bring wives to heal. This negates, I feel, the spirit of the word in favour of the law of the word. I bring empowerment and encouragement, at times from these very same scriptures, and offer suggestions for becoming aware of, and recognizing signs of abuse in the church context. It's time to take a look at what God means when He tells us the greatest commandment, to love one another.

> "The spirit of a person can endure his sickness, but as for a broken spirit, who can endure it?" (Proverbs 18:14, NASB).

Listen, if the spouse isn't prepared to admit or confess his secret domestic behaviour, there is little you can do that will change that. He's already going against a covenant agreement made between both of you and God. So, if he doesn't fear God, nothing you do will stop him. He has free will, but so do you. If Christians around you insist on refusing to fully understand and confront the depth of depravity, oppression, and control being exercised by your spouse, that doesn't mean you are doomed. There is hope. There is freedom. That freedom is contained in full view in the written word of God. It is a weapon that was designed to correct and protect you, not kill you spiritually. We are all ministers to one another of the new covenant that declares we are right before God, free of guilt, and set apart for a special purpose. That's right, you have been set aside for a special purpose. That purpose is not flogging yourself to spiritual death in an unevenly yoked relationship with a believer whose actions and words towards you fly in the face of what God has shown us of marriage. His marriage to Israel first, then the marriage of His son to the bride.

Don't endure it any longer. Beloved, start your walk to freedom. It's not your fault.

> "The offender's power is in the victim's silence. Together we can change the narrative" –Maya Meftahi (a domestic parental sex abuse survivor)

PRAYER

Lord, thank you that you love me with an everlasting love. Nothing can separate me from your love. Thank you for saving me, and setting me apart. Thank You that nothing is wasted, and all things in my life are being woven together to produce a reflection of Your goodness.

Help me to be a peacemaker, to see the truth and act on it. Give me the wisdom and courage to challenge unkindness, without fear of man.

I'm sorry that at times, I've just done church and haven't represented you very well. Sorry for my own thoughtless and hurtful words. Help me to consider the significance of every human I encounter, regardless of how they look, what they may have done or not done, and how they speak to me. They are fearfully and wonderfully made, flawed, and working their way towards their destiny. I pray in Jesus, Yeshua Ha Mashiac's name. AMEN

Chapter Three

Eesha Or Ayzer

"So God created man in His own image, in the image of God He created him; male and female He created them" (Genesis 1:27-28, NASB).

Ishsha, pronounced *Eesha*: wife, woman, significant other, a companion who is part of me. It's what Adam (which means human) declared when God made another human that was like him! It doesn't mean helper, because God had already said there was no helper found for him from amongst all creation. So God made the human into two parts from the flesh of the original, Ish and Ishsha. Interestingly man became Ish after Ishsha was separated from him! It is for that reason that marriage symbolizes a significant spiritual occurrence. It means that together husband and wife are made whole. What it doesn't mean is that without being joined to another human we aren't complete, that we are not whole if we are single.

You are made one with Christ, who came as flesh and then that flesh resurrected from the dead, corruptible to incorruptible. This was a prophetic sign that God and His image bearers would split in two, as Jesus left this realm, God the Father separated The Groom from The Bride. She had been chosen, had accepted the marriage proposal, and now anticipates His return, to consummate the marriage and take her to the home He's prepared! His created ones and He in unity—as one! So, we are complete in Him:

Entwining the essence-spirit of God and His manifest-flesh image in the earth! All sounds good so far! So where did it go so wrong? Why does marital abuse happen in more Christian marriages than secular ones? That, my beloved, is borne out by the experiences of many women I've encountered, and my own experience.

Dear Ayzer,

Have you ever felt that in your marriage all is not equal? You don't feel you are of one mind and heart? Whatever happened to the man I loved and married? My life is just a constant cycle of things I'm expected to do: an expectation for me to do everything. Why is he always so glum? Sometimes I feel that all I'm here for is to help him and forget my own needs. It's like I don't even exist!

Who controls the finances, are you allowed your own pot of money, no questions asked? Are you expected to perform your marital duty, when in fact you are exhausted or just don't feel comfortable doing these things when presently you feel no attraction for your husband? Are you expected to carry out sexual acts or listen to dirty talk that makes you feel degraded? Does he just carry on regardless of you being asleep, or saying you don't want to? Does he ever quote the Bible to you on the duties and role of a godly wife? Do you know there will be repercussions if you don't give him what he desires? Does he talk to you like you're a child, or like he's the boss of you? Sometimes it seems he has forgotten the duties and role of a godly husband, yet you dare not confront him with it. Have you been unhappy for years with no improvement, but have been encouraged to stay together despite what feels like a never-ending trial, trapped, and in fear of living a life of regret because you didn't try hard enough? Have you ever thought, "I seem to be the only one trying?"

Reading this book could possibly bring restoration, and it could even save your marriage! In this book, I'll be taking a good hard look at the "elephant under the carpet," which is women of faith who are being crushed by a husband who believes he's the boss. God put him at the top of the household hierarchy, bottom line, period, full stop–rubbish! Humans were given dominion over the creatures and land, but not dominion over fellow humans.

Let me clarify something. All humans were created from dust, else why would he say we were created from the dust of the earth both male and female? Humans are all equal in the Kingdom of God. Furthermore, when we entered into a covenant with Jesus, we were adopted into God's family, from which our earliest ancestors were cast out. We are sons of the Most High God called according to His purpose. Your purpose is far greater than being a helpmate, and a servant exclusively for one man. You are no longer a gentile, female slave, you are not a Jew, free nor male! We are told to submit to one another and God. It's not a one-way street. You are now restored and fully human. Not only that, but you are also fully spirit and in constant union in the heavenly realms. You are in Him and He is in you! What is done to you is done to Christ, and what isn't done for you, isn't done for Christ!

> And he said to the woman, "I will increase your trouble in pregnancy and your pain in giving birth. In spite of this, you will still have desire for your husband, yet you will be subject to him" (Genesis 3:16, GNT).

This curse was pronounced at the fall. However, we are not subject to this curse once we are in Christ, because Christ dwells within us. The same Christ that took the curse, literally became the curse, and then all curses were put to death (1 Corinthians 15: 42-58). Yet the curse can still afflict us if people act discordantly with the desires of God. The consequences of said behaviour can seem like a curse, not only because of our shortfalls but rather because of the fall. The consequences of an unsubmitted ruler are evident throughout scripture. Take Ananias and Sapphira in Acts 5:1-11.

Warning! There is a very real danger in agreeing with an unsubmitted spouse!

You are so loved by Him beloved, my beautiful sister. God is for you and not against you. You should not be suffering in silence. Stop it– just stop and think. Don't you wonder at the knowledge that you are so valued? He left His Kingdom, came in the flesh, and died in your place. If you feel you are being unfairly treated, or know that you are, please reach out, at least share your heart, and have some healing prayer. Read your Bible. Read this book. Get some balance, don't accept the word of a spouse that stops your freedom. If you have been praying for freedom and release you've got it, now lift your voice and wings to fly! It was for freedom that Christ has set you free. You aren't alone, you're in a frighteningly large statistic of 1 in 10 or 15 women at church.

Marital rape occurs in up to 14% of all Christian marriages! A social media post by Bushra Shaikh shows marital rape statistics for the UK, "Between 14% and 25% of women are sexually assaulted by intimate partners (spouse or boyfriend) during their relationship. Between 10% to 14% of married women will experience rape by their intimate partner in 2022." This demonstrates that Christian women who have experienced oppression are usually silent on matters of what goes on behind closed doors. Yet statistics show that domestic abuse in all its forms is allowed to carry on, unchecked, especially in Christian circles. I hope your reaction to that was the same as mine. I had to double-check and cross-reference. I find this utterly astounding, yet uncomfortably, I felt exonerated. There was always a niggle of, "Am I the only one," or "Was I right to leave the marital home?" The situation was made worse by the inability to show to the world that I had real and valid reasons for seeking separation, which I'd finally decided. I felt the need to show people I hadn't just walked out because I didn't love him anymore, or that he was just difficult. One can hardly shout out to the world that there is sexual abuse in the marriage; or that there's mental abuse, not least because largely, that is still not acknowledged even in the world at large. It can even be perceived as something you can work through or as an exaggeration! The usual advice follows, and oh boy, if you say he has a porn addiction and then leave, you could be thought of as being "over-sensitive" or unforgiving. The list can go on. I have walked this road a very long time! Our circle of friends even cajoled me into trying to' love' him again, "Go on, hug him. Tell him something you respect and admire about him." I may have done the same in their shoes, who knows? The fact is, it's not that I didn't love him, it was that I started loving the me that Yeshua/Jesus loved and died for.

Unless you've experienced it directly or walked with a friend through the entire journey, you can't understand the subtlety of a gradual erosion of your principles under the influence of a master manipulator. This is especially true if you've been groomed by other manipulators throughout your life. A person cannot realize how deep childhood and previous failed relationships affect emotional responses. You will let a person walk over you when all you want is to be happy and for the conflict to disappear. You can't see and escape when you're not fully aware of how imprisoned you are. Not just by the behaviour of a misguided spouse, but by your own insecurities and fears.

It was always me who expressed my discomfort while in close proximity or withheld affection, so it looked as if I was the one with a problem. Our church community where I live is very interconnected, which is great, but I felt I had no one I could talk to openly! Even worse, once I'd told a few people some of what was going on, I felt I ought not speak to yet more. Not until that day

> "Faith is not just a matter of hope and optimism; it's a matter of courage. It's the courage to believe that God will do what He said He would do, the courage to make peace with being misjudged when others don't understand the path you're on, and the courage to stick with it, even when you don't understand the details yourself."
>
> – Andrena Sawyer
> Author and Christian Entrepreneur

while out walking with my friend, I went straight in at the deep end. I just snapped after she'd said something that triggered me, and it all came tumbling out.

In the next few chapters, we're looking at statistics, cultural norms, cultural and historical grooming and Christian attitudes towards troubled women, divorced women and women who complain about iniquity within the home.

PRAYER

Lord God, I come to you humbled by your grace and mercy, which I see demonstrated throughout your word, and around me. Lord God, I sometimes can't see that working out in my life. Please help me Lord, to see what I can't see, accept what I do see, and take decisive steps to guard my heart and mind against the schemes of the enemy. Please Lord, send me friends that I can talk to, to disclose this burden that I carry. Lord, I feel like I'm just here for everyone else, and that I don't really matter. I know Lord that I am yours, born again for a purpose, to be loved by you, to love you and make you known. My life may look like it's ok from the outside, but inside I'm feeling "thin." Please, Lord, give me the strength to take action, so that I may be a sign of your goodness, love and mercy. In Jesus, Yeshua Ha Mashiac's, name. AMEN

Chapter Four

Disturbing And Acknowledging

The LORD regretted making human beings on the earth, and his heart was grieved." (Genesis 6:6)

In my life, I've personally known many women who have remained in abusive marriages for a whole lifetime. I have changed their names to protect them. Take Tamsin whose alcoholic husband abused her behind closed doors, or Maria who refused to leave or divorce her abusive alcoholic husband, or Sylvana, who divorced then remarried Dave, then divorced him a second time only to take shelter under my roof as he stalked her, at times becoming violent towards her even though they were apart. Meanwhile, Debbie's husband sold their home and made his wife and three children homeless. Sonya was escorted out of the county by the police, fleeing her abusive police constable husband! There's Sue, whose drug-addicted husband convinced social services he was competent to have custody of the children and subsequently abused his daughter after leading her into drug addiction. Ellie's husband was dealing with his porn addiction, though he'd had church leaders at several churches over the years for accountability. All the while expecting her to role-play acts that were painful, humiliating, and degrading. Coercing, manipulating, and dominating with controlling actions daily until there was virtually no resistance left seems to be the consistent pattern. I know of three more victims, who revealed marital abuse to me since writing this. That's ten women whom I personally know. All Christians.

I could go on, as sadly these accounts of people known by me first-hand are plentiful. It's time this stopped. The silence, the uncomfortableness, awkwardness, and the biblical legalism that pervades should never leave a woman feeling helpless, hopeless, confused, silent, and often made to feel responsible for his well-being at the expense of all else.

Unfortunately, the evidence isn't obvious, even to a trained eye and ear. So let me give examples of how women living with abuse can be invisible:

- ❖ An unhappy person tends to fly out of the building to avoid idle conversation. The operative word here is idle.
- ❖ Without sincere connections and community in a body of believers, conversation tends to stay at the everyday level of weather, church, work, and the kids.
- ❖ An unhappy person often carries an invisible "don't talk to me" sign or is someone who can remain aloof and invisible.
- ❖ A victim of abuse won't usually attend mid-week Bible studies or events. Sometimes they won't turn up on a Sunday, though the spouse may still do so.
- ❖ A victim may not offer to help on rotas, clearing up, or conversely may keep themselves very busy serving!
- ❖ An unhappy person living in an unstable environment will often look down at the floor, or a book, leaflet, etc.
- ❖ They may be considered moody.

I'm not plucking things out of the air; these are tactics I've used. The reason behind it, personally speaking, is that I felt as if I would say too much or speak to someone, and it would get back to my husband and then there would be trouble. It wouldn't be that

I was speaking ill of him, just that he'd always correct me or pull me up on something. If I did intimate that there were issues at home, my husband would find that people started treating him differently as if he'd done something awful (which he had, but as far as he was concerned, he hadn't) or they began avoiding him. My firm belief was that I wouldn't be believed, or worse, would be judged and rejected for "talking about my husband."

In short, it wasn't a safe environment. And I'm not just talking about one church congregation. I actually attended three different places of fellowship alternating between them. This was more because of my belief that "church" is the people of God, and not just about a single group that worships in a particular building: not because of my unfortunate circumstances. Though it did mean that the people that became true friends were actually all from different "bases", so it greatly increased my opportunity to make meaningful relationships with those I began to trust, because they trusted me.

The problem with this thought process is that I was unable to make meaningful connections and friends, thus learning to trust some of them enough to confess my circumstances. And then, when I eventually made a few friends of course, I found there was pitiful little they could do to ease my suffering, so I'd stop talking to certain friends, and then find a new set of friends and start again. Subsequently, I was then convicted of being a creaking gate, telling far too many people things that shouldn't be shared widely. So, for a while, I vacillated between telling and not speaking about it to anyone at all, retreating once more into myself.

Fortunately, I stumbled upon a few who counselled me, by listening and offering prayer support and even next step suggestions. Unfortunately, on one occasion, a friend said to me some very unwelcome words, which I find hard to forget: "Well you can hardly blame him, after all, you went along with it." That really hurt–but not everyone understands the complexity and mind games played out by an abuser, not even the abused, and often for many years. This put me back a few steps, and I began to retreat and stopped talking to others. But thankfully two or three kind souls listened carefully and drew me out; so much so that I blurted out all the worst and most sordid details. This started my freedom walk. Sound familiar?

A problem shared is a problem halved. - Old English Proverb

To bring balance, I have to acknowledge there is an increased awareness of the issue of pornography within the church at large. It is indeed a step in the right direction. This is something the church seems to be addressing and is taking seriously, particularly with the increase in men's groups and ministries. I know it is addressed in Christian magazines, which are often available at churches. It is also discussed through YouTube channels and vlogs. This massive and seemingly complex issue is debated and discussed openly. With the increase in social media presence in the last fifteen to twenty years, this is sure to remain an important subject that needs honest and frank discussion.

I also acknowledge the increase in preaching from the front, and that sermons are not just exegesis of certain scriptures or chapters. I do note that these tend to be pointing people, generally, in the right direction; but is it preventing them from going in the wrong direction? Why do they go in the wrong direction? What leads them to do it in the first instance? These are the issues that require more commitment than just preaching and teaching. Why is abstaining from marital lustful sex not talked about? There are so many Christian books and teachings on what kind of sex is ok, and what may not be. Granted, the Bible leaves plenty of scope here, or does it? I'm sure there is already a book out regarding this, so I will park that right there.

Disturbing And Acknowledging

Whilst I am thankful for this acknowledgment, that "Houston, we have a problem," has been heard and that the rescue mission has been undertaken. The problems that surround this, the impact on lives, careers, children, and the underlying cause plus the way the church is done these days often leave plenty of scope for the offender to continue with no accountability structure or honesty. Churches are often too small, too big, inexperienced, or just unaware of the situation that prevails unrelentingly. The issue is made far worse by the presence of smartphones carried around everywhere we go.

An Example Of Damaging Careers

My husband, before we were married, unbeknownst to me, had lost his job due to being caught looking at pornography at work. I found out many years later that he had been indulging in porn in his first marriage too, so it may well have contributed to its demise. He subsequently decided to go self-employed, so when we got married, he'd often spend hours in his office "working". One day I caught him with his pants down masturbating to images he rather hastily tried to close before I reached across to the keyboard to see what he's just hidden, and in disgust, I walked away. That was the third time I'd caught him 'at it' and each time he gave assurance it wouldn't happen again. Needless to say, it did. He never worked a full-time job in all the time we were together, and now doesn't work at all and hasn't for eight years. He used the excuse that as we were carers for our disabled child, he couldn't get a job. Strange, because I did, and for the first seven years I was the only carer, plus housekeeper, and handled all the finances! That caused a grudge because though I'd asked him to take an interest in the finances and contribute, it was I who ended up with this burden. I'm certain he simply lost confidence in himself through guilt perhaps, or self-hate—hardly surprising really. He couldn't churn out jobs fast enough, and so had a small clientele of two regulars, and an occasional extra job thrown in. His earning capacity was damaged, as he couldn't in all honesty charge for all the hours, as some were "misspent." He refused to upskill and said he'd preferred the old programs he used. Quite likely, the old PC probably couldn't cope with new programmes, and he probably didn't want to get rid of that PC anyway, due to the images he kept on it, so eventually the work dried up.

Of course, I hadn't ever put all of this together. I couldn't see the wood for the trees so to speak. Some years later, his mum passed away, and he drew an income from the inheritance, giving up work completely. At fifty, he declared he was retired. I, meanwhile, five years older, continued working to bolster up the spiraling cost of living. I've realized since then that he would keep tabs on me, probably because of his perception of women, which was perverted by what he was engaging in. He had become quite controlling, and maybe he thought I was up to no good! After all, if he was, he could reason, I could be.

So back to the acknowledgment of the problem of porn. Of course, another matter is that whilst singletons are committing a possibly lesser sin, with lighter consequences, in that it only directly affects themselves, for married men the results are usually devastating. It causes unhappiness in the marriage bed, and conflict in the wider home environment. The contrast comparison of these two sides of the single versus married, regarding the use of porn doesn't make for good topics to talk about in the church. Whilst men may well confess to this, and seek to become accountable for porn viewing, with accountability partners, there is little in the way of dialogue with the spouses. Another thing to factor in is that not all abuse is of a sexual nature, nor is all sexual abuse due to pornography. So dealing with this particular issue does not seem to raise the other, which is the adulterous nature of all porn use. It is making porn a god whom they interact with, submit to, and spend time with, rather than God.

Again, the church has been fairly forward-thinking, in that a lot of the churches now conduct marriage courses. This is acknowledging that there should be some peer supervision and guidance regarding marriage. Something that had sadly died out long ago when people stopped honouring God and didn't train their children in the way they should go.

The fact remains, there are many forms of marital abuse, and possibly pre-marital abuse, such as, when people are engaged in a meaningful relationship, and/or are engaged to be married. This can range from, overstepping boundaries, to spiritual abuse in a sort of, "this is what I expect from our relationship/upcoming marriage" kind of way; by the way of using scripture to exert male authority or headship. Another is the subtle use of coercion with a resultant slip-up, and/or emotional blackmail to drive a woman into the marriage covenant. This just continues into the marriage, and once the ring is on the finger, this will escalate, or become a cyclical occurrence. Conversely, it may subside for the literal and perhaps prolonged honeymoon period to re-emerge later.

Not to mention that whilst any abuse may not be an occurrence at present, there will undoubtedly be those who have endured abuse as a result of a spouse who has an affinity for porn or has had an upbringing in which the parents had an unhealthy relationship. It could also be a single parent who had a string of failed or unhealthy relationships. Some people end up church hopping, whilst others just stop attending. For the abuser, it's so he can hide what is going on, and the woman can be forced to stay at home, or if church hopping, can't get to know anybody. This is often facilitated through manipulation or control. There is usually little real relationship between infrequent or non-attenders and therefore accountability is missing.

There are things we don't talk about to protect people, and many wouldn't understand, or simply, people are often too busy doing church instead of being church: no public confession, no restitution, no protection. Even if a man is brave and humble enough to confess the sin of porn addiction, he is extremely unlikely to confess the effects of playing out the acts portrayed in these images. Much less acknowledge that having cyber-sex is actually adulterous. Yes, if a man is masturbating to the still or moving images of a woman either masturbating or having sex with others, it's adultery. He is worshipping the sex act and not God. He is having sex with someone who is not his wife. If I hear one more Christian woman counsel another to not be unevenly yoked in reference to embarking on a relationship with an unbeliever, I may just have a tantrum! Too many times, I've heard a woman telling another that to marry a non-Christian would be to become unevenly yoked. That makes me angry, because many lovely Christian women would love to have a good husband, and many a good husband has been overlooked because of this scripture. The scripture I refer to in 2 heathen, untrustworthy, that believe not, unbelieving faithless, infidel. A person who professes Christ can also present with these traits. It says here, "without Christian faith" and yet a woman can find a man, who though he doesn't know Christ, may well work to Christian morals. As we see in these pages, many men who confess Christ, do not. However, I'm not advocating marriage to an "unbeliever" but may just be hinting at marriage to a closet believer who just hasn't met Jesus yet!

Listen, people can be more unevenly yoked to a believer! A believer who is unkind, unmerciful, and irresponsible is in every way more harmful to a woman and his children than an unbeliever who is honourable, kind, loving, and takes responsibility for himself and the home. Which is better a man, who says he will stop but

Disturbing And Acknowledging

doesn't, in this case a Christian or one who says he can't stop but does–the unbeliever? The first doesn't change, but the second does because he's come under conviction. The first yells grace, and the second whispers– it just didn't feel right.

Men can't have their feet in both kingdoms! If smoking was going to kill them–they'd stop smoking! If jumping out of a plane with no parachute is insanity, why do they continue free-falling yelling grace? They need to fess up, grow up and show up. They are in the army now advocating for the vulnerable, the weak and the voiceless. Not taking advantage of the vulnerable, damaging them until they are weak and silencing them through manipulation, scripture, or fear tactics. If they would acknowledge they have a problem, there would be something to work on. It seems that women always take responsibility and eventually, if not sooner, acknowledge that the relationship is in fact unhealthy or that, many receive the label of rebellious, or worse a "Jezebel." To repeat those famous words, "Houston, we have a problem"-still!

PRAYER

Lord God, I come before you now with reverence and in humility. Thank you, Lord, that you are Father to the fatherless and protector of widows, you set the lonely in families and you lead out prisoners with singing. I'm sorry when I've not done what I see you doing, even within the walls of my own home. Help me to have open eyes to what is occurring right under my nose, and ears to hear what you are saying to me. Please Lord, equip me to be the answer and not contribute to the problem. Please heal my heart from wounds yet give me a heart of flesh instead of stone, that my heart can break for what breaks your heart. Help me to pray earnestly for those in silent anguish and help me in times where I feel my heart is breaking. I accept that pain is something I will experience here on earth, but it only lasts for a night, and at some point, joy will come. Give me your oil that I may have gladness in my heart again. Your JOY gives me strength, and your spirit raises me up to fly high as an eagle. Lord have mercy on your oppressed women everywhere, and make me an instrument in this battle.

In Jesus, Yeshua Ha Mashiac's name. AMEN

Chapter Five

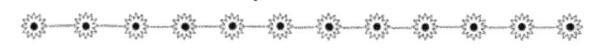

Is It Abuse Or Oppression?

You say, "Why does he not" (as in not listen to our prayers). I'll tell you why; because the Lord was witness between you and the wife of your youth, to whom you have been faithless, though she is your companion and your wife by covenant (Malachi 2:14, NLT)

The Lord works righteousness and justice for all who are oppressed (Psalm 103:6, ESV)

According to Crisis England and Wales: 400 abuse victims commit suicide each year, 200 on the same day they visit the hospital for domestic abuse injuries.

In the UK during the COVID-19 pandemic, there were 105 intimate partner deaths on a report by the National Police Chiefs Council, this accounted for 48.9% of all domestic homicides.

Abuse is defined, according to dictionary.com, to treat in a harmful, injurious, or offensive way, to speak insultingly, harshly, and unjustly to or about; revile; malign. It represents at its most basic, a flagrant disregard of another. Inflicted on a person, abuse is the *attitude and thoughts* of a person leading towards an action directed towards another– a heart matter. Out of the wellspring of the heart issues all things. I've connected it with the biblical word oppression, which is the exercise of authority or power in a burdensome, cruel, or unjust manner.

A scenario:

Shirley and Tom were shopping at a grocery store, Tom pushing the trolley. She put in a bottle of wine, and he gave her "one of those looks." Shirley put it back on the shelf. In the next aisle, he put in a bottle of Whiskey and again looked at her. Shirley said nothing and quickly turned away to carry on down the aisle. At the till, Shirley asked Tom for the bank card and paid. They walked out to the car in silence, packed the groceries in, and drove home. As they were putting the shopping away, a light conversation started, about what they were having for dinner. She was tired and didn't want to spend ages cooking, especially as Tom liked his meal at 7 p.m. prompt. The trouble started when his meal choice was going to take too long. She stood at the sink peeling vegetables, holding back tears. Tom had gone upstairs, but he could come down so silently, he mustn't see her cry or it may all explode again, and dinner will take even longer. She just wanted to sit down and relax. By the time they'd finished dinner, Shirley had cleared up the kitchen. She was so tired she decided to go on to bed early, leaving Tom watching tv, and as she left the room she heard the drinks cabinet open. Much later she heard him as he noisily got ready for bed. She didn't move a muscle even though she was now wide awake. Perhaps he'd leave her to sleep. Her heart was racing and she froze as he got into bed. She prayed silently to God, please Lord let him go straight to sleep. Just then his hand was on her shoulder, and his legs wrapped around hers as he pulled her onto her back.

Afterward, he rolled away and fell into a deep satisfied sleep. "I think I'm losing my mind, soon there'll be nothing left of me," she thought to herself as she rolled to the edge of the bed, tears streaming silently. It was some time before she managed to fall into a restless sleep. Strange visions and dreams swirling around in her head, of walking into church covering up her bruises. But of course, some wounds can't be seen.

I'm very disturbed, a righteous anger has been stoked within me, especially so in recent times as I hear more and more frequently of women who walk with God, women of faith who are being or have been in an abusive marriage. In particular, where the abuser is a self-confessed Christian. Often the traumas and humiliating acts are endured, not least because there seems to be a dearth of avenues for support. These women in the pursuit of protecting their family children and the church, are often silent.

Silenced.

Silent and dealing with all that life presents whilst burying their pain, humiliation, and anger.

Sorrow may last but a night but joy comes in the morning. Little comfort after years of abuse.

The Oxford English Dictionary defines "oppression" as: Prolonged cruel or unjust treatment or exercise of authority. The state of being subject to oppressive treatment. Mental pressure or distress.

> "He who oppresses the poor shows contempt for their Maker, but whoever is kind to the needy honours God" (Proverbs 14:31, NIV)

In the Oxford English Dictionary contempt is, "the feeling that a person or a thing is beneath consideration, worthless, or deserving scorn." Dr. John Gottman, clinical psychologist, has identified contempt as the number one predictor of divorce. After four decades of research on marriage and divorce, he wrote, "Contempt is the most destructive negative behavior in relationships." He goes on, "It's virtually impossible to resolve a problem when your partner is getting the message that you're disgusted with them and that you're condescending and acting as their superior."

So, how does God feel? When a man treats a woman with contempt, he treats God with contempt at the same time! This action of the husband towards the wife deems God as disgusting. As scripture says, if you oppress the poor, you show contempt for your maker. Oppressing people must in itself be born of contempt. Again, the Online English Dictionary defines abuse as: use to bad effect or for a bad purpose; misuse, treat with cruelty or violence, especially regularly or repeatedly. As an adverb: the improper use of something (i.e. alcohol), or cruel and violent treatment of a person or animal. So within the very definition, cruelty and violence are present.

Abuse is a hard thing to define because unless it's at the top end of the scale, which is more overt and domineering, such as forced sex, non-consensual penetration, and physical violence. Almost every action and inaction can be a form of abuse. In the scenario above, between Shirley and Tom, most of those behaviours in isolation, and the absence of Shirley's reactions, could read and be viewed as perhaps they were normally a happy couple and they'd just recently had an argument or even no argument at all. It's just he had a better suggestion, in choosing the whiskey instead of the wine. Perhaps they were splashing out or preparing for a Burns Night with friends! (Burns Night is a Scottish tradition where haggis is eaten alongside a glass of whiskey!) Perhaps, it could be deemed that Shirley might have had a drinking problem and her action needed a reminding look. Perhaps, she had left her bank card at home and needed to use his? You could read any of it in innocence not seeing the whole picture.

So, what if I think I'm in an abusive marriage, what are the signs? To be frank, if you need to ask that question, the answer is that you probably know that you are! If your husband is doing, saying, and being something that does not honour God, on a day-to-day basis, he has forgotten his covenant, and who God is.

If you feel like you don't matter, then he is probably not lifting a finger to change that. If he is expecting too much of you, then he's forgotten that you are God's daughter, a royal princess.

THE BLAME GAME

Like Adam regarding Eve as the one who led him astray, or led him into sin, so often a woman is accused to deflect from their deep, often unrecognized feeling of inadequacy and failure.

Discernment is key here because women are not above being the abuser. Both parties must be heard and feel they are being believed. Another trip-up point is that in the case of relationships, where there has been abuse, there can be counter-tactics that can appear as abuse. So, a woman who is suffering unfair treatment may end up speaking disrespectfully about her husband. This can be due to many complex factors. One is that it is not safe to show any display of disregard at home, because of the unsavoury consequences, and so it can seep out into the safety of numbers theory; even more so if the persecutor is out of earshot, but in the room. The fact that there is a disregard at all should raise a red flag. You cannot respect a spouse who spitefully uses you or disregards your needs all the time. Respect is mutual, but also so can disrespect. A woman is often made to feel complicit as coercion is a modern-day phenomenon within many relationships. It is more covert than manipulation, but no less damaging. It is one of many useful tactics to gain control over an unsuspecting or susceptible victim. It can be interpreted by a selfish controlling person as willing consent. As I said earlier, often when women go for counselling within the church (and sometimes out of it), they are often equipped with tools on how to help the situation but not how to get out of the situation. Meanwhile, the men are not equipped because they often don't see or admit that there is a problem. So once again, it falls to the woman.

So many women are forced to look after the home, the husband and hold down a job. This leaves precious little time to consider their own needs, and so a cycle of poverty of spirit continues. We become orphans. We wonder why God allows things to happen to us, because *if* He was a good Father, "He would rescue me". You can even get angry with God or blame him for the situation, especially when one believes they've been called to that marriage by God himself.

> "Have nothing to do with the fruitless deeds of darkness, but rather expose them. It is shameful even to mention what the disobedient do in secret. But everything exposed by the light becomes visible—and everything that is illuminated becomes a light"
> (Ephesians 5:11-13,, NIV)

It's time for us to be brave. It's time for us to understand what counts as abuse and what doesn't. Sometimes it can be a very fine line. We are not excommunicated from Jesus' church nor God's Kingdom because of divorce. The Malachi 2:16 verse has been twisted. Here it is again in two trusted versions:

> And you ask, "Why?" Because even though the LORD has been a witness between you and the wife of your youth, you have acted treacherously against her. She was your marriage partner and your wife by covenant. Didn't God make them one and give them a portion of spirit? What is the one seeking? Godly offspring. So watch yourselves carefully, so that no one acts treacherously against the wife of his youth. If he hates and divorces his wife," says the LORD God of Israel, "he covers his garment with injustice," says the LORD of Armies. Therefore, watch yourselves carefully, and do not act treacherously. (Malachi 2:14-16, CSV)

> Yet ye say, Wherefore? Because the LORD hath been witness between thee and the wife of thy youth, against whom thou hast dealt treacherously: yet is she thy companion, and the wife of thy covenant. And did not he make one? Yet had he the residue of the spirit. And wherefore one? That he might seek a godly seed. Therefore take heed to your spirit, and let none deal treacherously against the wife of his youth. For the LORD, the God of Israel, saith that he hateth putting away: for one covereth violence with his garment, saith the LORD of hosts:

therefore take heed to your spirit, that ye deal not treacherously. Ye have wearied the LORD with your words. Yet ye say, Wherein have we wearied him? When ye say, Everyone that doeth evil is good in the sight of the LORD, and he delighteth in them; or, Where is the God of judgment? (Malachi 2:14-17, KJV)

PRAYER

Lord God, please hear my prayer. At times I don't seem to be aware of what is going on around me, yet I know what is going on in the world. Please open my eyes to the lost and hurting, inside and outside the church. I ask you to show me my blind spots, the places that have become hard through the knocks of life. If I have retaliated to wrong, please forgive me, where I have accepted wrong, please forgive me, I acted or didn't act from a position of fear of man. Please help me to overcome this fear and give me the courage to speak and act with boldness where I can see oppression. Help me to be a voice crying out in the wilderness and bring the body of Christ back to the central message of the cross, freedom in Christ. In Jesus, Yeshua Hamashic's name. AMEN.

Chapter Six

Did God Really Say?

"My sheep hear my voice, and I know them, and they follow me" (John 10:27, KJV).

In this chapter, I want to clarify the scripture that apparently says "God hates divorce," which we've taken to mean divorce is not an option. This is then further 'rubber-stamped' in the New Testament, or is it?

I believe God does hate divorce, but that isn't the primary message in this verse. We all hate divorce, because it reveals a lot of trouble has happened, and divorce in itself causes upset and disadvantage. Divorce should never be treated lightly, and effort should be made by both parties to find a workable and mutually acceptable solution.

So often, we inadvertently take responsibility for our spouse's happiness and behaviour. And here's the shocker - often the woman is counselled to change her ways, in order that the husband changes! Yet, we know we can't ever change someone else, only our own selves including how we respond to situations. Our mindset needs to change, and for that, we need to understand the word of God and the heart of God.

I'm not equipping you to "leave your husband in three simple steps" and equally it is not about "how to please your husband in three easy steps!" I'm not about reinventing the wheel and this book is not about teaching and guiding. It is about revealing how much Father God loves you, values you and desires you. In ways that no human can ever express.

The focus of this book is edifying (building up) and releasing women. Not least from the bondage of being subjected to pleasing the man, whatever the cost. It is also about releasing you from the letter of the law and the written words of the Bible. Misinterpretation and taking scriptures out of context have been utilised for centuries to bring compliance to millions of earth dwellers.

Why are you paying the price? Marriage to some, if not all, is considered a big sacrifice. Jesus paid the cost. He exemplified the union between a husband and wife and nailed injustice and bondage to the cross.

You don't need to nail yourself to the cross, just carry it!

Carrying your cross is about remembering the journey Christ made before nailing all sin onto it. The journey He took because He kept in His mind your redemption, which gave him the joy, the very joy that lay before Him was your redemption! It cost Jesus. He paid for your freedom! Think of it as carrying the memory of what He paid for your freedom!

Yes, it's all about submitting to God's will which is to see you set free and flourish! It means only doing what you see your Father doing, and He "does" setting captives free, healing, and bringing peace! Am I speaking your language yet? If in doubt, remember what God did with the languages at Babel. He confused the languages as man was making himself as god. Is something confusing you? Is that because your man is taking the place of God in your life? When Yeshua, Christ, took that to the cross He took man's submission to Satan and as a man submitted it to God! He rose to new life, to give you new life, the holy written word, and then Holy Spirit came that we may all speak and understand the language of heaven, the language of God our Father, the love language of the Father.

You are His child, a citizen of His Kingdom, and His bondservant! How can I be all three, I hear you ask? Good question! If we are "just" His child, think how arrogant or entitled we might be– My daddy, the King! We'd be running around in the Kingdom as if we owned the place, which is where citizens come in. A citizen lives alongside others who all have equal rights to security and happiness. We all live respecting and honouring one another because if you don't, that causes the fabric of that community to rip. Now if we are "merely" citizens, but not children, that would mean we are subject to the rules of the ruler and have no rights if that is what the ruler decides. Our ruler is our dad, so that's ok because we do have rights. That makes us a huge extended family! Then, we are bondservants. A bondservant has rights but chooses to stay committed to his/her master. Free choice, but serving out of respect, honour, and love.

You are free. As a result of being free in your mind and heart, you, or those you counsel, can access healing from the ravages that manifest physically in the body that are a result of years of crying, depression, disappointment, and hopelessness (the Bible calls this hope deferred).

Please Note: I'm not talking about the ravages of physical and sexual assault, for that you may require prayer ministry or treatment from the medical sector. If you are being physically harmed, seek help in the secular realm is my immediate advice, as soon as you can and, if possible, take a believing friend or confidante along with you. Plan ahead and ensure young children are safely away from the home before any confrontation of physical harm or undesired abhorrent sexual behaviour, and again, a witness, a recording, call someone you trust and leave the phone on loudspeaker. Be wise, calculate the right moment, and don't be sucked into a heated discussion that began with heightened emotion.

There are many books that have been written to help women overcome difficult relationships with their husbands, and many more books suggesting how to please your husband. Let me reiterate I do not intend to repeat, nor indeed endorse what is already available. I'd need to read multiple dozens to be able to make recommendations. Sadly, those I was given over the years, didn't serve me well. I won't name them here. The responsibility, it seemed to me, primarily relied on the woman to keep the man happy. Pray for him, please him sexually, and dress nicely. This is likely because women are usually the most likely to seek and accept counselling/support. Perhaps because they're the ones needing help. They are shouting "Save me, help!" What they really want is for someone to help them make sense of the way they feel, and to reconcile that with the word of God. The whole word of God. Not just scriptures that teach them how to be good, pleasing, or perfect models of servanthood. The whole counsel of God, for all scenarios.

There are also many similar books teaching church leaders and counsellors. Yet how many men actually go to a leader about domestic unrest? Especially if deep down they know it's because the wife won't seem to accept his leadership style. Perhaps they feel that as they rule at home, and the church leaders rule at church? No accountability is required!

Not skirting around the issues that affect us in our homes, I'll expose, underpin, and underline the truth behind scriptures that have been used to keep women in their place whilst bringing light to scriptures that will enable you to understand that God really does hate abuse, whilst dispelling the myth that God said in His word, He hates divorce. God loves His daughters! God does not favour sons over daughters. We are one, equal in importance and He loves you. He wants you to be cherished, protected and presented as an unblemished, beautiful bride. To shine radiantly as a reflection of His glory! To raise offspring that are the same reflection of His glory! You're His bride–first and foremost.

Let's break down these verses that are quoted in Malachi 2:13-17 Please read it in your translation, then read it here in a wider context:

And this second thing you do. *God is responding and referring to more than one thing here, referred to earlier.*
You cover the Lord's altar with tears, with weeping and groaning Whining/moaning because He no longer regards the offering or accepts it with favour from your hand. *God appears to have not responded favourably to these people. This can be equated with, why doesn't God hear my prayers and heal me?*
Why? **Because the Lord was witness between you and the wife of your youth, to whom you have been faithless, though she is your companion and your wife by covenant.**
Now he explains the purpose of two becoming one. **Did he not make them one, with a portion of the Spirit in their union?**
What was the one God seeking? Godly offspring. *Marriage is for humans to multiply and take dominion, all of God's children in relationship and rulership with Him through Godly leadership.*
So guard yourselves in your spirit, and let none of you be faithless to the wife of your youth. For the man who does not love his wife but divorces her, *(talking about a man not loving his wife and instead divorcing her)* **says the Lord, the God of Israel, covers his garment with violence, says the Lord of hosts. So guard yourselves in your spirit, and do not be faithless.**
You have wearied the Lord with your words. But you say, "How have we wearied him?" by saying, "Everyone who does evil is good in the sight of the Lord, and he *(the Lord)* **delights in them** *(still or in spite of)*.**" Or by asking, "Where is the God of justice?"**

KING JAMES VERSION

Malachi 2:14-16:

Yet ye said, Wherefore? Because the Lord has borne witness between thee and the wife of thy youth, whom thou has forsaken, and yet she was thy partner, and the wife of thy covenant. And did he not do well? and there was the residue of his spirit. *[In her]* But ye said, What does God seek but a seed? But take ye heed to your spirit, and forsake not the wife of thy youth. But if thou shouldest hate thy wife and put her away, *(divorce her)* saith the Lord God of Israel, then ungodliness shall cover thy *(the perpetrator's)* thoughts, saith the Lord Almighty: therefore take ye heed to your spirit, and forsake them not *(your wife)*.

KEYS OF THE KINGDOM HOLY BIBLE

Malachi 2:11-16:

Judah has dealt treacherously, and an abomination is committed in Israel and Jerusalem. For Judah has profaned the sanctuary of Yahweh that he loved, and he has married the daughter of a foreign god. Yahweh will cut off the man who does this, the awakener and the answerer, from the tents of Jacob, and him who offers a meal offering to Yahweh Sabaoth. And you have done this again covering the alter of Yahweh with tears, with weeping and with crying out in that He *(GOD)* does no longer regard the offering, nor receives it with goodwill at your hand. Yet you say 'why?' It is because Yahweh has been a witness between you, and the wife of your youth, *against whom you have dealt treacherously,* although she is your companion and the wife of your covenant. And did He not make them one. Yet the vestige *(remnant or residue-still has a bit of the spirit of God in him, enough to know that he is doing wrong).* And what of he who was looking for a seed from God? So be watchful over your own spirit, *(be aware)* and let nobody deal treacherously against the wife of his youth. For Yahweh, the Elohim of Israel, has spoken of hating divorce, and Yahweh Sabaoth has spoken of hating him who has carried destruction on his clothing. So be watchful of your own spirit, and do not deal treacherously.

Check out the AMP, NIV, NASB, and other versions. There are many other places where there are verses about divorce, and I will deal with them later.

I am not an advocate of divorce. I am an advocate of not enabling, helping, aiding, and abetting, an abusive, controlling, self-obsessed, bossy, demanding, narcissistic, self-centered Christian boy-man to continue unchecked. If you can't identify anyone amongst those adjectives, then count yourself blessed. Please note I use those as describing words– adjectives. I don't use naming words or nouns. These words are not who they are, but descriptions of their attitudes and mindsets, which are the root of their actions and words. If you allow your spouse to continue in ways that are harmful to you, the children and himself he will separate himself from God. He is behaving like an unbeliever! Do you want your spouse, the head of your household, and the father of your children to be separated from the grace and goodness of God? Nothing can separate them from the love of God, but behaving like an unbeliever means we and God will regard them as an unbeliever. There are biblical grounds for that too. It's amazing what you can learn from the bible!

This scripture informs us of the outward signs of an inward mindset, a mindset that sets itself up against the knowledge of God. God does not give us a depraved mind, but a sound mind:

> Furthermore, just as they did not think it worthwhile to retain the knowledge of God, so God gave them over to a depraved mind so that they do what ought not to be done. They have become filled with every kind of wickedness, evil, greed and depravity. They are full of envy, murder, strife, deceit and malice. They are gossips, slanderers, God-haters, insolent, arrogant and boastful; they invent ways of doing evil; they disobey their parents; they have no understanding, no fidelity, no love, no mercy. Although they know God's righteous decree that those who do such things deserve death, they not only continue to do these very things but also approve of those who practice them. Romans 1:28, NIV

Even more important, God may not heed your husband's prayers, "Likewise, ye husbands, dwell with them [your wife] according to knowledge, giving honour unto the wife, as unto the weaker vessel, and as being heirs together of the grace of life; that your prayers be not hindered" (1 Peter 3:7, KJV) Moreover, regarding your prayers, God does not change a person's will. Your spouse has free will to make choices when presented with a set of options, so your requests to God regarding changing your husband are likely met with a firm "No". Your husband has to recognise his fallen unrepentant state before he can move in the right direction. If you are the only person who knows, well, there is a big problem! Because if his behaviour towards you is ungodly and disrespectful, but he doesn't acknowledge it, it makes the process way more problematic. You see, the Bible gives us guidelines for disputes, but if the injured party doesn't feel brave enough, or is in fear of recriminations, it becomes a dead-end street. Therefore, the biblical process, or as they say in court, *due process*, meaning a principle of fairness in all matters, cannot happen.

I'd like to clarify that in order to reach the point whereupon I could write and speak to you with clarity. I have undergone counselling over the years and more recently, spiritual heart healing. It is vital that I come to you speaking not from a place of

Did God Really Say?

pain and vivid memories but of peace and a healed heart and mind. I focus on solutions derived from shining light onto scripture and I do not focus on problems and pain, to ensure it doesn't become a cathartic rerun or over-sensational sharing. I share here openly. I have forgiven all wrongs against me– a few times actually! I've reached a part in my story where I can say that apart from the civilian legal process of justice, I want no vengeance or harm to fall on the perpetrators. Any estate or financial unfairness is laid at the feet of my Lord. He is the God who provides, and He's never let me down.

I've researched both the scriptures and many books relating to this topic of abuse in Christian marriages: Joined support groups, communities and listened to podcasts and vlogs from both the United States and the United Kingdom. This is no walk in the park, bullying within marriage, especially amongst believers, is one of society's best-kept secrets. I'm about to blow the lid off of this can of worms particularly, but not exclusively here, in the United Kingdom. If you're intrigued, grab a coffee, get yourself a comfy seat and come with me as we delve into our first conversation.

Bear with me then, as we look into the root of mankind ruling and submitting. We need to look at the whole picture to get a true perspective and deep understanding of our divine creator who shared consciousness amongst all creation.

"Then God said, 'Let us make man (kind) in our image, according to our likeness. They will rule the fish of the sea, the birds of the sky, the livestock, the whole earth, and the creatures that crawl on the earth" (Genesis 1:26, CSB).

God doesn't want any of His people subjugated, trapped, unhappy, silenced or controlled. Not any of His humans. He never said to rule over each other.

What Genesis 1:26 doesn't say is dominion over man (kind)! So that includes you, your daughter, mum, sister, or friend–not anyone! The abomination of slavery was instigated by mankind, not God. Likewise, with animal sacrifices (Isaiah 1:11) and divorce, God tolerates or allows it, because our authority was handed over to the devil; because of that, we wait with groans for the return of our King. Just like all sin, there are always consequences to mankind doing things its own way. A third of the heavens' angels left because they didn't agree with God. He desired family, fellowship, and unity, but they wouldn't submit to Him, and the consequence was expulsion.

Another expulsion happened with the first chosen people, as they also chose to disagree with God. They were banned from a paradise that gave them eternal bliss life. Now out of the garden, they were eternally separated from God. He didn't want them in an eternal state of perpetual sin, so they were cast out into a finite realm, our time-locked planet. Then He made a way for His people, called by His name, to return to Him. It took a while in unfolding, but it happened before time, on the mercy seat, in His Kingdom. That meant it could not be undone by anything or anybody. Not by the fallen angels, and not by the fallen humans. It was done by God Himself.

In the next chapter, I will reveal the history of God's boomerang people! He throws them off into the sunset because of their lack of submission, trust, faith, and belief that He had their backs; but, they just kept returning to Him, usually after being chastised by prophets or over-ruling nations. Eventually, they decide, as a nation by now, that they want rulers of flesh. I guess they wanted someone they could identify with. Someone like themselves. So they obviously didn't fully comprehend that they bore the characteristics and likeness of God within, probably because, through their lack of submission, they trusted in the doctrines/teachings and ideologies of fallen angels, and Nephilim the giants of old. It was obviously a struggle for centuries until Jesus appeared and changed it all.

Did God Really Say?

It's still a challenge today for many believers to trust in the Lord our God with our everything! The multitude of teachings and bible translations can be confusing and conflicting. Opinion seems to win over accuracy. Many of us just blindly believe what we're told and what we read, without cross-referencing. Who has time for that? Especially women with jobs, kids, husbands, homes, and church duties to consume our every hour and spark of energy. Yet we seem to find time to read extra-biblical books at times. You wouldn't be reading this right now if that weren't true!

So why do we find the written word of God so hard to understand? I wish there was a simple answer, but there's not. Taking on board what others have come to understand, who are from our culture, time, and belief system can reframe things, focusing on particular revelations specific to their own message. This was exactly what the writers of the Bible were doing. So, it's not a great sin. But it's wise to read the scriptures quoted in several versions, and if possible, a Strong's Concordance and even commentaries. At the very least take a look at some online translations, and not ones that all agree. Look into some that say it differently. Don't ever just take their word for it.

PRAYER

God, I submit my thoughts to you, please take them and make them clean, and honouring to you. I want to hear your voice, so please hear mine as I ask you to speak to me at this moment. Help me to know your thoughts, to seek out your heart in the words that have been written and copied down through the centuries. I trust your word, the living word Jesus, Yeshua Ha Mashiac, as by your spirit you guide me into truth and righteousness. Lead me towards the truth, in non-biblical writings and books too, Lord you can speak to me through anything. Please Lord make me a vessel of your power, love and a sound mind. I rebuke the spirit of fear in Jesus, Yeshua Ha Mashiac's name. AMEN

Chapter Seven

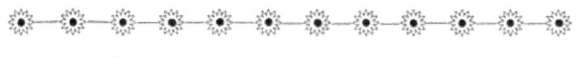

Marriage And Divorce

"Bear one another's burdens, and thereby fulfil the law of Christ"
(Galatians 6:2).

It is not lost on me that when Jesus began His ministry, it was at a marriage celebration! I say "began" loosely, as it was his mother, Mary, who instructed Him to miraculously sort out the wine problem at a family wedding! This miraculous exposure of the Kingdom of Heaven must have caused enough of a stir that He would not be able to hold back from continuing what was now started! The wedding at Cana is central to His message. His message is that we're the bride and He's the groom, the new wine is flowing profusely, and then He went to His Father's house to prepare a room for her, and to await the day He can return when His Father says to go and collect His wife! The celebration of a wedding was a whole village affair because a marriage, after all, needs a good supportive community around them. Celebrations build relationships, as does organising one! I'll leave that there for now, as I could write all day about the significance of the bridal paradigm!

Suffice it to say, two things of absolute importance must emerge from this chapter on marriage and divorce. Covenant and mutuality are essential to the Kingdom message that Jesus preached. We are His beloved bride, whom He brought into a covenant relationship, where we are no longer divided but one with Him. He is one with God, therefore we are one with God. So there is a mutuality within that relationship. So what is done to the Bride is done to Him. What is said to the Bride is said to Him. What is withheld from the Bride is withheld from Him. If we are doing and saying bad things, others as servants, piling expectations onto people, and being legalistic or unkind, we are badly representing the very spirit of God within us.

One of the biggest issues I have is that our marriage customs have been shaped by men, as in the male sex, not mankind. In Roman times, there was a written code for marriages called the Roman Rite, most of which made up the one in the middle ages– the eleventh-century. It was called The Sarum Rite and was one thousand years after Christ. This in turn became incorporated into the Book of Common Prayer in 1549. Yet the newest scriptures of the Bible were written just over one hundred years after Christ. The vows we often say when getting married weren't customary in biblical times. The whole 'with my body I thee honour' or anything like obeying. In fact, in one of the simple rites, the man actually commits to "worship" the wife! That surely can't be right? So what, in the Bible constituted a marriage covenant?

The marriage in biblical times, commenced when a man asked a woman to marry him, having sought his own father's and her father's approval, and she subsequently agreed. The woman was allowed to agree or refuse! Then there was a short ceremony including both their fathers and close family only. The bride price, which most of you won't have heard of, was an insurance policy for the woman that if she was widowed or deserted that money was for her to live on. It is intended to protect the woman, primarily by establishing the man's financial obligations to her in case of the aforementioned scenarios. Usually at this ceremony, both the man and woman would have time to express their expectations and

Marriage and Divorce

wishes, so the other could know and agree to them. This was known as a Ketubah, which is the standard marriage contract that Jewish law requires a groom to provide for his bride on their wedding day. It is intended to protect the woman, primarily by establishing the man's financial obligations to her in case of divorce or widowhood. Then the woman would go back to her home, and the man to his father's home, where it was then customary for the man to build a home attached to his father's house—Prepare a room for her! At some point, of the father's choosing, he announces to his son that he felt he was now fully prepared, and that he could go and collect his wife! There would be a week of ceremonies and celebrations involving the whole village, after which the wife was taken back to her husband's house. So they would be legally married at the first ceremony and yet not consummate the marriage until after the actual collecting of the bride when the father gave the nod! Can you imagine any man nowadays waiting up to a year or more to consummate his marriage? So you see, our view on biblical marriage has been skewed over time, becoming a blend of centuries of the church and then secular culture. Many people live together before getting married, small wonder that it goes wrong when the husband-to-be can't even wait until the public ceremony and agreement (aka wedding), witnessed by an accountability circle. A husband should be accountable to a tight knit community. Where there is no accountability, a culture of disrespect can creep in.

> If you are in the statistic of 40-45% suffering sexual assault or forced sex, or the 15% suffering nonconsensual sex (which is rape) or violent rape; your faith can be crushed in the bedroom.

When a spouse treats us with indifference, and then at times we bite back and in so doing we are both disrespecting God and our vows. If we bite back though we cause escalation, and so usually, we back down! Thank God for

Jesus, eh? He taught us that love is the higher path. I believe that a woman who may bite back, at some point, starts not to bite back anymore, resorting to the demure humble position of accepting her lot, leaning on God's grace, and hoping someone notices something or that the husband realises his wrongdoing. But as the harsh confines of an unhappy relationship spiral, usually quite slowly and subtly at first, we find ourselves drifting away from Christian activities, meetings, and the Bible. If you are in the statistic of 40-45% suffering sexual assault or forced sex, or the 15% suffering nonconsensual sex (which is rape) or violent rape; your faith can be crushed in the bedroom. Your salvation, though secure, seems an empty promise for the elite few, and you disappear into silent obscurity.

> "But to the married I give instructions, not I, but the Lord, that the wife is not to leave *(depart/separate from)* her husband but if she does leave, she must remain unmarried, or else be reconciled *(to change mutually, change their minds)* to her husband, and that the husband is not to divorce his wife." *(divorce has been construed from af-ee-ay-mee=S-G863- the word divorce is not in the list of words, the word af-ee-ay-mee, means any one of the following to send forth, cry, forgive, forsake, lay aside, leave, let alone, put away, remit, yield up)*
> 1 Corinthians 7:10-11, NASB

Here we are talking about a woman who has left without divorcing, so, of course, she must remain unmarried because otherwise, she'd be committing bigamy by taking a second husband, as she's not divorced from the first one. Furthermore, if she leaves, but changes her mind and he accepts her back, he is not to forsake her! The word written in Greek means to leave or send away. The reason Paul wrote this is that here, he's referring to couples who have separated! Therefore if they were only separated, and then went to live with another man or marry another man, she'd be committing adultery (as she wasn't divorced, just separated). Same for the man, if he was only separated from a

Marriage and Divorce

previous wife, not divorced, and he subsequently married another woman, he'd be making her (the second woman) an adulteress.

Thayer's Definition: to send away, to bid going away or depart, of a husband divorcing his wife, to send forth, yield up, to expire, to let go, let alone, let be, to disregard, to leave, not to discuss now (a topic), of teachers, writers, and speakers, to omit, neglect, to let go, give up a debt, forgive, to remit, to give up, keep no longer. You see, the problem here is you have a definition that goes beyond the remit of the word. In this context what Paul is not saying is divorce, but separation.

Matthew 5:31-33, NASB

Verses 31-32 It was said, whoever sends his wife away let him give her a certificate of <u>divorce;</u> but I say to you that everyone who <u>divorces</u> his wife, except for the reason of <u>unchastity</u> makes her commit adultery; and whoever marries a divorced (ap-ol-oo'-o) woman commits adultery.	**Divorce:** *ap-os-tas'-ee-on-* separation **Divorce:** *ap-ol-oo'-o* (G575 and G3089)- free fully, relieve, release, dismiss (reflexively depart) or (figuratively) let die, pardon or (specifically) depart, dismiss divorce forgive let go loose put (send) away release set at liberty. **Unchasity**: por-ni'-ah- Pornography
Verse 33 Again, you have heard that the ancients were told, "You shall not make false vows but shall fulfill your vows. But shall fulfill your vows to the LORD."	**False vows:** ep-ee-or-keh'-o- to commit perjury: forswear self. **Vows:** hor'-kos her'-kos- a limit that is sacred restraint (specifically oath). NOTE: Interesting that the writer of Matthew says the word apostasy meaning separation which has been written in as divorce! Greek apóstas(is) = desertion.

75

Mark 10:2-9, NASB

Verse 2 And some Pharisees came up to Jesus, testing Him, and began questioning Him whether it was lawful for a man to divorce his wife.	**Divorce:** (apoluō): free fully, relieve, release, dismiss (reflexively depart) or (figuratively) let die, pardon or (specifically) **Divorce:** depart, dismiss divorce forgive let go loose put (send) away release set at liberty.
Verses 3-4 And He answered and said to them, "What did Moses command you?" They said, "Moses permitted a man to write a certificate of divorce and send his wife away."	**Divorce:** (ap-os-tas'-ee-on): separation NOTE: Their answer was to say that Moses said they could separate from the wife. If she didn't have a certificate of divorce she couldn't remarry, as in those times, she was effectively the husband's property. He, of course, could marry others, by man's rules, a man could have many wives! Perhaps it's because that was the custom before they became God's people and so He permitted it. Remember at Eden, after the fall they weren't God's people because they'd accepted the leadership of Satan. The problem here though, is that the Pharisees didn't misunderstand divorce. It was that they misunderstood marriage.

Marriage and Divorce

Verses 6-9	NOTE: There is a physical law that combines with God's spiritual law when two humans become one: a male-female under God's covenant of becoming whole with each other and Him. A chord of three strands! God wanted communion with His creation, so He created the man Adam (adamah) and breathed His breath (ruach) into him. The woman came from man, then God rejoined them all back together in a mystical union: the man, woman, and Himself. The first humans to have some of God's spirit (ruach) through an amazing process of a common union—communion.
But from the beginning of creation, God created them male and female. For this reason, a man shall leave his father and mother and the two shall become one flesh. so, they are no longer two, but one flesh. Therefore, what God has joined together, no person is to separate.	

Divorce, He allowed because of the hardness of their hearts—cruelty creates calluses. Once we have joined together in a covenant between God, our husband and ourselves, that's it, we are always one, unless someone breaks the covenant. One spirit. Just as well, there's no marriage in heaven, only glorious aeons in the presence of God, at one with Him throughout eternity!

Remember, neither you nor God have broken the marriage covenant. The unbelieving spouse has. If you had broken it, I doubt you would be reading this book! If your husband acts towards you in an ungodly manner repeatedly and unrepentantly, he is an unbelieving spouse. He doesn't believe in God, because he doesn't respect God, nor His written word. Just because he can talk the talk, doesn't make him a believer. Just because he has an outward appearance of walking the walk, doesn't make him a believer. It's who he is in the confines of his home, with those God has given into his care: wife, children, an elderly parent, and even animals in his care! In the Bible, the shepherds knew their flock, on Ligonier.org they write, "When Jesus introduces the figure of the shepherd in John 10:3, He does so with imagery that suggests the shepherd's intimate knowledge of his flock. In calling to his sheep, the shepherd does not utter merely a general cry for all of his lambs to come. Instead, he calls them by name. He has such deep love for and knowledge of his sheep that he calls for them individually."

He tends his flock like a shepherd: he gathers the lambs in his arms and carries them close to his heart; he gently leads those that have young" (Isaiah 40:11 NIV).

Did you know, by the way, that in the Bible there are woman shepherds? In biblical times, many women shepherded flocks, "Rachel came with her father's sheep for she was their shepherd" (Gen. 29:9, NIV). One of my favourite women, Zipporah, was a shepherd, "Now a priest of Midian had seven daughters and they came to draw water and fill the troughs to water their father's flock" (Exod. 2:16, KJV). She married Moses after he fled Egypt *(he left an Egyptian wife and child(ren) behind)*! These matriarchs of Israel both met their husbands at wells where they led their flocks to drink. During the course of their daily work, the contact occurred that led to their marriages and many more years of caring for flocks.

Possibly half the shepherds in Jesus' day were women! Anyway, I digress!

On the website, Enduringword.com they write, "There are some that neglect the whole counsel of God and say that God never allows remarriage after divorce. When we see what the entire Bible says on the subject, we see that if a divorce is made on Biblical grounds (adultery or abandonment by an unbelieving spouse), there is full right to remarry." The issue we have, if any, is to fully understand adultery and abandonment by an unbelieving spouse.

Marriage and Divorce

If your spouse is treating you with disregard, like a slave, expecting you to perform all given tasks and ungodly tasks or sex or eroticism, *(which is different from intimacy or into me see)*, anything contrary to God's design for marriage. If he forces himself on you, gets angry, shouts at you like you're a child, or is violent, he is breaking God's marriage covenant. In other words, he shows no regard for or even contempt for God, he is an unbeliever.

The Bible says in Matthew 18:15-17, NLT:

If another believer sins against you, go privately, and point out the offence. If the other person listens and confesses it, you have won that person back. But if you are unsuccessful, take one or two others with you and go back again, so that everything you say may be confirmed by two or three witnesses. If the person still refuses to listen, take your case to the church. Then if he or she won't accept the church's decision, treat that person as a pagan or a corrupt tax collector

If he has departed from the marriage covenant, the covenant with God, he has **abandoned** you too. But as I said earlier, it may not feel safe to take two or three witnesses because of repercussions once back behind closed doors.

PRAYER

Father God, Lord, you are my redeemer, my father, brother, and husband. I am not rejected by you. I am your child, not an orphan. Please help me to understand your written word and the words you speak directly into my spirit. I am fearfully and wonderfully made, in your image. My command from you is to know you and make you known. I confess, at times I've allowed the way people are towards me to be a reflection of who I am, both positively and negatively. I'm sorry, I am who you say I am. Whether I'm single or married I am still yours, your beloved. Please reveal to me how a husband loves a wife. In Jesus, Yeshua Ha Mashiac's name. AMEN

Chapter Eight

Root Problem To Solution

"Watch over your heart with all diligence, for from it flows the springs of life"
(Proverbs 4:23, AMP).

Just as the world seems to be constantly coming to an awareness of the effects of climate change, the same could not be said about the culture in which we live, our homes, and our communities. Our social climate has become very dangerous with each new generation suffering as the social norms cause a greenhouse effect of toxic morals. As each generation kicks back and rebels against the injustices of their time, the moral compass no longer points to True North but instead follows the stronger magnetic pull of the world and its worldly ways.

Sadly, much of the established church instead of being counter-cultural aims at being friendly and relevant at best to culturally complimentary, embracing the current movements or ignoring them in the hope that it's another storm the church can weather! Too many broken women become outsiders, leaving the church in droves. Gradually the undesirable separated and divorced stopped attending. The communities became fractured and unbalanced as the church community became a sort of elite club of happy families and couples embarking on new married life! The attendance drops, and not many notice the women who sit on the edges. Church life went on regardless.

In the noughties and into the twenty-first-century, the church refocused and revived. However, the institution of the church was getting revived but not church society as a whole. Heading into the noughties people in new movements were celebrating being drunk in the spirit and having gold dust and holy oil manifesting. People were full of joy and reveling in this new era and yet in my forties, I felt something was still so very wrong within the body. What was missing was genuine relationships amongst the fellowship who met on a Sunday, and once midweek. Then we came into the era of healing, counseling, and sometimes even classes! There was a glimmer of hope–or was there?

What the church needed, and the world too, was kingdom principles based on the Bible and other uncanonized contemporary writings. In ancient times God wasn't just a thing you did on Sundays and a midweek study; He was woven into the very fabric of their lives. So, what the church and world need is a core deep kingdom moral compass that points to God, seeks God, and submits to God. I will state here that I have been quite fortunate in the fellowships I've been part of. Yet, after the first marriage went bad, I did it all again. For me, it wasn't the church per se, it was me. My understanding of scripture, and within it the guidance of humans by God, was being coloured by my relationship with God, which to be honest, was more of a "help me" and an "If I worship you through the pain, maybe it'll all go away." I hadn't been discipled–one-to-one. I had been taught from the sermons, and they don't usually cover topics such as infidelity, cruelty, pornography, or aggression!

Nowadays, there are multiple Bible translations available, plus a plethora of online apps. As more and more go back to the original language to translate from, plus the older versions are more readily available to purchase, (some even online). People are gaining a clearer understanding, not only of the words within but the history, archaeology, and prevailing customs and cultures of those times. I have found the internet to be a valuable portal through which we can, with intentionality, find a balanced understanding of words and scriptures in our Bibles. It was through deeper study of keywords that I have been able to pinpoint where a simple traditional teaching or scripture has gradually come to be portrayed as meaning something that entirely suits certain echelons of society. The very thing that I used to defend when debating with non-Christians, was the fallibility of its human writers. I have after many years of study discovered just that! But, when I say study, I mean deep, thorough, and unbiased research using all means available. Such as Google, Wikipedia, various ministries, podcasts, and even a couple of unorthodox teachers of biblical accounts.

I still completely trust the word of God, brought to us by humans inspired to document lineages, rules, poetry, histories, letters, and personal revelations. I just don't always trust those who declare theirs is the ultimate translation! Balance, discernment, and time are required to sift through the Bible. To be directed by His spirit is a good start. The solution, I propose, is discipleship. Discipleship that is firmly, scripturally based, not based on exegesis and opinion. Dialogue is the key, not monologue.

THE REASON

Women who stay in an abusive marriage do so for a variety of reasons. Quite often, the number one deeply indoctrinated belief is that God hates divorce, so don't get divorced. That scripture is so deeply misquoted that it has become embedded into society, law, and non-faith cultures. Though this trend is gradually reversing. Have you ever thought to yourself, "If I persevere and show tolerance, the relationship will improve?" Another aspect could be, "It wasn't like this in the beginning, so maybe this will pass."

The longer humans spend in an unhealthy and unrewarding environment, the more normal it becomes. We're really good at adapting to adversity to the point that it's just a normal way of life. If one is kept in that frame of mind, thoughts of freedom are a rare concept.

Adversity will oftentimes make us resilient and stronger but occasionally we unknowingly fall into the trap of believing we're strong for tolerating when the truth is that resisting injustice is the action of a person who has conviction and shows true strength.

In my time, I've encountered many others across varied walks of life. Within different cultures and environments, they have stayed under the control of an abuser. This situation isn't just in heterosexual relationships nor exclusively within the covenant of God-ordained marriages, within which the victim can be coerced by well-meaning Bible-believing people to stay and not break that covenant. Financial control or instability, commitment to a mutual organisation, and even parents or the environment we grew up in can play monumental roles in our compliance.

So, let's unpack some of these things. Are you willing to deep dive with me?

POVERTY AND FINANCIAL INSTABILITY

A few years ago, I began looking into my family tree. During my research, I spoke to many of my relatives. I found this a most rewarding task as I began to form a sort of relationship with my relatives from the past and made new or stronger affinity with living ones.

One conversation that was particularly poignant was about my maternal grandmother. It was about her marriage to a drunkard who was violent. She had lost her parents around the age of sixteen or seventeen and so at that young age married this man. This was 1917. Eventually, despite the hardship ahead of her, my gran fled with some of her four children, (she'd also lost three during pregnancy and childbirth) and lodged in a rooming house,

Root Problem To Solution

which in today's terms would be a bedsit with shared communal areas. One account was retold and it caught me unawares, it was that she "hosted" men of an evening after the girls were asleep! I initially thought no, not my gran. But quite quickly, I realised this was post World War 1, in a deprived area of England not long before the time of the Jarrow marches, which were yet to come. The overarching climate was poverty. It was no place for a single mother. She needed to earn so that she and her children would survive—and survive she did! It was whilst she was living here she met a man also lodging there, who used to make soup for her children. He would become my grandad. In time, the Second World War started, and so with limited choices, my Gran went with my grandad as he moved around England to work on the docks during the war period. My mum and oldest aunt were born in Newcastle and London respectively, and shockingly they were born out of wedlock! After my gran's first husband passed away in the nineteen forties, they were able to get married and went on to have two more girls.

It was through my mother that I discovered her daddy was a proud but violent man who liked his drink, often going straight to the pub on payday. He was violent to both mum and my grandmother and life was very tough for them as gradually work for grandad dried up completely leaving them on the breadline. Add to that, grans deteriorating health, which resulted in mum being removed from school aged just fourteen to look after the home, her mum and three younger sisters. And yet I was brought up by my mum who was a single parent and when my stepdad moved in, what I saw her do was exactly what I was groomed to do, which was to serve the man in every way, food when you get home from work, etc. It seems, even though she was trapped into looking after the whole household when she was young instead of moving away from that role, she stepped straight into it as an adult

Father wounds are created in a person when the father has wounded the child/young person by cruelty or absence. This can be caused by external or financial pressures. This could be physical, mental, emotional or a combination. There is a saying, hurting people hurt people. The reason I took you on this journey into my past, is that we can often look back at those behind us and think that life is so much better now. Yet, it is my firm belief that these unhappy circumstances are still going on right under our noses even within the very core of Christianity. So veiled, so unspoken and yet it still happens.

> Financial, mental, or emotional instability and poverty can both be a cause and a symptom. A sort of chicken and egg scenario

Financial, mental, or emotional instability and poverty can both be a cause and a symptom. A sort of chicken and egg scenario. Certainly, in my own direct experience, my spouses' behaviour led him down a path of online pornography and masturbation, cloaked in lies and subterfuge. From the outset of our marriage, he didn't put any income into the running of the house. Everything was left to me. I balanced the books, did all household chores, cooked, etc. There was a huge financial burden on me. He was unwilling to contribute in any way. The scales were grossly out of balance. Fortunately, I was skilled and financially stable before he appeared on the scene, or else it would have been very different. So for us, it was the case that the symptom came first. His symptoms exposed a deep problem that affected every area of our lives together. It underpinned everything. In that scenario, no one is fulfilled.

If a man is trapped in a cycle of pornography and therefore unfaithful, he cannot step into his kingdom identity. Not only that, but the deceit and control which hide his weakness begin to control his spouse leaving her also unable to fulfil her kingdom purpose. Thus, both are literally of not much use when it comes to the Kingdom.

Another example of this is a couple where there is control, especially when there's financial control that causes financial famine. Even though women have worked as far back as time itself men seem to find themselves at odds with their spouse that's earning more than they are; or conversely, are on a low income. Often the running of the household, such as paying bills, fall to the main earner. This can cause a kind of chain of command which can be seen as one person being in control causing the other to feel they have no say. A toxic mix even in the most settled of marriages.

"Submit to one another out of reverence for Christ" (Eph 5:21, NIV)

FEAR – False evidence appearing real.

Researchers have found (to their surprise) that, "deeply religious people stay in horrible marriages longer and endure far worse abuse than average" (Baskerville). There are many ways that fear comes to us. In the previous chapter, I dealt with the scripture that has been misquoted that can instill a fear that we somehow lose our salvation or our place in the church by leaving and/or divorcing a man who is un-Christ-like. I'm going to discuss other ways that fear can keep us in an unhappy place.

I have been married twice for a period spanning thirty years. In both marriages, I stayed despite the awful conditions in which I lived. From day-to-day, I lived in fear of reprisals, of behaviour and of the consequences of leaving or denying the husband his marital rights. In both marriages, I was forced into the sexual act which under any other circumstance would be called rape.

I have endured the merry-go-round of repeated bad times followed by a season of an indeterminate period of good times and of what seemed at the time genuine sorrow or repentance. Each time you hope that this is the time it really has changed. So you can be frightened that if you leave you may just miss something that could be good. Also, fear of depriving the children of their father's good behaviour or of exposing their fathers 'other side' to them.

When you get past those barriers and you start realising that you're going to have to share it with somebody, probably at church, a fear rises up in you that they won't believe you because your husband is so charming and nice. Finally, if you have got that far by telling somebody at church, you go for counselling and they tell you to bear with them, to speak with them about the things you're unhappy about, and to not deny them their sexual rights. Then, the biggie, when you have managed to tell somebody who understands and believes in your plight, instead of telling you to stay with him, they say that they will stand by you if you decide to leave. After I had that conversation, I was more scared than I'd ever been before because I knew there was no going back and there would be reprisals, hardships, and struggles ahead.

Don't be encouraged to stay with an idolator (nor encourage women to do so).

ASSIGNMENT

What is our part? Our part is to first lay boundaries. Second, to get healed hearts. The third, is to be coached/discipled in scripture. The fourth is to speak up!

I don't believe it to be coincidental that when you really read the scriptures how often God speaks to and through women, despite the apparent patriarchal societies of the ancient world. There are many fascinating glimpses when you know how, and where to look!

Jesus Yeshua continues doing what He sees His Father doing, takes up not only the cause of women but seeks them out,

Root Problem To Solution

commissions them, and even submits to them! Just reflect on that for a moment, take thirty minutes, grab a drink, and think about Jesus's attitude and respect towards women.

All men, except the first, came through a woman. *Ishsha (eesha)* is the first recorded word for the human that was not man. In fact, man both male and female were called man (as in human). As I mention in a later chapter, the word used for woman is debatably not the same root as man. *Ish* means strength. Woman is from a root meaning weaker vessel. Before she appeared, God said he'd make an *ezer kenegdo* which means a helper who is against him. It really interests me that God would make and call her a helper who is opposed perhaps opposite him, yet when he wakes up from his deep sleep, *ish*, the strong one, immediately names her "weaker vessel." I suppose in order to strengthen her there was an acknowledgment of her vulnerability. Perhaps his deep sleep and surgery had caused him to feel that she'd been the cause of himself being made weaker (purely my conjecture of course)? Perhaps the jury is still out on the root of the two words which sound so much like a connection– *Ish* and *Ishsha*. Again, as I said elsewhere, the human was put into a state of non-awareness, and God made the one into two halves, so she would have stood before him in that garden when God presented her to him: opposite him, across from him, beside him. Perhaps the man feeling incomplete, because he's been made into two, was feeling weaker? We can't hypothesise on something that far back, and let's face it; to most people, especially with science, biology and all, to think we can more appropriately describe how the human race came about nowadays, is not smart at all. I mean, apes into man? Does that sound any better?

I guess a woman in the throes of labour and childbirth is vulnerable and needs protection, not to mention when the sexual act is taking place the man is usually dominant and "in control" all whilst a woman generally is about as vulnerable as any human can be, apart from aforementioned childbirth, where both mother and infant are extremely vulnerable. I guess God knew what He was doing when He designed us! I mean, if you've read this far, we should perhaps agree to let God be God! We've done that so far, especially if you've been trapped in a horrid cycle because of misquoted scriptures, then you must agree that your trust in God and His written word is of utmost importance to you. Surely that could be why more Christian women suffer marital abuse and for longer than women of no faith? We were trusting God but ignoring His wisdom and His words directly into our spirit, which keeps us trapped in a cycle where there seems to be no way out.

So, shall we get back to the garden? We all know what happened next; the vulnerable woman got tricked. Where was her man? Well, he was beside her, when she reasoned with him that they'd become wiser if they consumed the fruit (lie), that he'd been told not to eat, they'd know everything, and hey– downward spiral. Now they were both vulnerable, both weaker, and both working their way back to the Father, who in their error, they had rejected. They gave legal right to the imposter. They became orphans.

In this, we accepted the fallen worldview that we were less than and should accept that we must submit to men as the head because that is what it says in the word. Men, meanwhile seem to have forgotten the part about the hard unyielding earth. Instead, it seems they decided that other humans must yield their free will. That became the teaching of the church, which seemed the right thing, so surely blessings follow? Hmmm—the slave trade banked on that, and women— well— much like the children they bore, they became seen but not heard. The gloves were off. For centuries, women took it; until one day, they didn't and that was in the world. In church, it was a whole other ball game. Women couldn't attend the temple, then they couldn't show their hair, then they couldn't

Root Problem To Solution

speak in church, they could only teach women and children, in the home, they must submit, and that is where, like a rabbit in the headlights, I froze. I chose to read that, hear that and live that, all without question! Well, that may be a teensy, weensy lie! I may have rebelled a little at times!

We now turn 180 and walk for the sake of future generations in the way set before us. So if a spouse uses his position of authority to carry out unbiblical and non-kingdom acts and behaviours it's time to oppose him. To walk in the opposite direction. If he uses his superior strength to subdue us, we must go to the church leaders; and if they don't act, go to trusted friends or outside organisations, and if in danger separate and relocate.

We must realise that we are role models for our children. They don't do as we say, they do what they saw modelled. And so history repeats itself and resentment boils up into radical societal movements where people are disowning their gender or only mixing with their own gender. For those who stay heterosexual, they resort to believing the lie that they are worthless, as are the foetus's of the unborn. Gender mutilation and feticide have become a modern epidemic.

Ladies, women, eeshas, ezers, it's time to take the assignment of opposing sexual perversion, bullying, control, lying, male entitlement, manipulation, and violence. Oppose the coping mechanisms of addiction to get through another day: the alcohol, prescription drugs, TV, internet depression, and anxiety.

If God is for you, who can stand against you? It's going to be tough, yes, there will be times of doubt and confusion. But remember, because of your action and boundaries, the generations after us may re-align with Kingdom principles. When they see that injustice, addiction, aggression, domination, manipulation, and control are tackled the right way. If not resolved, they can walk away head held high, and refuse to submit to the thought that they are worthless. I believe that God has always had a redemption plan for his Eeshas–His girls. It got set into motion as Mary submitted to God and became pregnant outside of the customary parameters before they consummated their marriage. The saviour who brought us salvation came through her. He had a mum and sisters and his heart towards women was displayed openly. Let's step into him and step up to heavenly realms.

Army boots on–Ezers, assemble! Let's take this land for future generations. Let the Eesha of God rise up in each of you. He's got this, and so have you!

PRAYER

Lord thank you for being Yehovah Yireh, the Lord who provides, you supply my every need. That may come through my job, my spouse, the government, but ultimately all the money, gold and silver are yours. In order to live a life fully surrendered to you I acknowledge that a portion of my income needs to go to helping the poor and needy, and also those in the mission field. You even give seed to the sower! Help me to be wise with finances without developing a poverty mentality. Just because I've had to go without, or make tough choices in times of lack, doesn't mean you don't love me, and care for me. Sorry, when being a Christian has diverted my gaze from Your biblical principles, and onto signs and wonders that are in the absence of the gospel message. Please help me to remain rooted and grounded in love. Lord, I want to be brave and not fearful, but at the same time be wise to the moves of the enemy and those he's trapped in a snare. My fight is NOT against flesh and blood but against powers and principalities. I come to you in prayer because that is the way to fight a battle, primarily. Prayer is a two-way conversation, so help me to know your voice. In Jesus, Yeshua Ha Machiac's name. AMEN

Chapter Nine

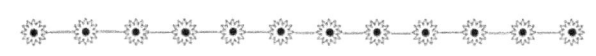

Spiritual Abuse

"He has qualified us [making us sufficient] as ministers of a new covenant [of salvation through Christ], not of the letter [of a written code] but of the Spirit; for the letter [of the Law] kills (by revealing sin and demanding obedience], but the Spirit gives life" (2 Corinthians 3:6, AMP).

So many times, the Bible was used by men in my life in order to correct me, usually to serve their own needs. However, I became pretty adept at misinterpreting scriptures and taking one-liners out of context for myself! In some ways, I believe I did so because of the scales over my eyes. The place my heart was at, and my unrenewed mind coupled with an orphan spirit, meant I served a coup de gras on myself! An orphan believes, "I'm not as important and valued as my husband." My heart believed that I had misunderstood the meaning of the word love. After all, there are many types of love! My mind told me, "I need to concentrate on making sure the children are my priority, that the house is clean and tidy" I had no time for searching out the meaning of life, no time for meaningful Bible studies with others, and even when we did Bible studies, it was as a group, with others at housegroup. Usually, the topics were pre-chosen by whoever was leading, so searching out answers as to why I felt the way I did, why my husband was the way he was, or even what the writers of the Bible were attempting to convey was so not happening!

Spiritual abuse is a form of emotional and psychological abuse, which compels the hearer.

It is characterized by a systematic pattern of coercive and controlling behaviour in a religious context. Spiritual abuse can have a deeply damaging impact on those who experience it. It is a skillful use of the word of God to justify self-gratification by the protagonist. It can also be wielded by immature Christian counselors who have failed to detect the true depth of what is occurring behind closed doors. It can feel like a subtle form of coercion, because it brings you into agreement that you and God together can fix the problem. To obey to the letter of the law, compels you to obey errant teaching which can be taken out of context, or mistranslated. We sometimes hear of historical abuse done by those representing places of authority in the church. I'll give an example; with the advent of tele-evangelists, gifting and tithing on the back of over-excited men of God exhorting you be obedient to the word, "God loves a cheerful giver" and "give and you will receive" or "give and we will pray for you," was often pointed out as the most heinous of crimes involving using the word of God to convict people into an action they had not already decided upon.

This type of abuse may include: manipulation and exploitation, enforced accountability, censorship of decision-making, requirements for secrecy and silence, coercion to conform, inability to ask questions, control through the use of biblical texts or teaching, requirement of obedience to the abuser, the suggestion that the abuser has a God-given or God ordained position of superiority. Often isolation is used as a means of punishment.

The use of spiritual truths or biblical texts to do harm is another form of spiritual abuse which can be teamed up with other desires of the oppressor-abuser for extra power. Sometimes battered wives are told that God wants them to be submissive to their husbands. As an exaggerated example, people could quote, "do not think of yourself more highly than you ought" (Romans 12:3, NIV) to suicidally depressed people. These are examples of abuse–even if what is said is a quote from the Bible, even if submission and obedience are in a general sense virtues. It is the twisting of good things in order to do harm that is so disturbing about this kind of abuse.

For more information on spiritual abuse, please see the references in the back of the book.

Another matter that is very dangerous is the gradual waning and occasional questioning of your own faith. Does God really love me? How can God allow this to happen to me? I'm not good enough to be loved by God, because I feel soiled and dirty. Is this what God meant when He said submit? If so, then I'm not sure that's the same God whose son Jesus cared so much about women.

Over a long and painful marriage, faith can be crushed. Our bodies become vehicles for another person to derive sustenance and gratification, and what we need is irrelevant. Our mind, hearts, and spirits become crushed. Then, we tend to read verses about how God loves a broken and contrite spirit and identify with it; or a woman bearing up with dignity. We might hear that God hates divorce. I suspect that the figures for marital abuse are greater within Christian marriages because most of us simply stay put. We stay put and keep quiet. Often there will be one or two confidants who will ever know the truth. So for the sake of the church, the spouse, the family, you accept unkind at best, brutal at worst, marriage. All the while crying yourself to sleep whilst crying out or ranting to God the Father who seems to have turned His face from you. God, it seems, is not concerned with your heart, your body, or your marriage. The husband is supposed to be submitted to God, and so because all seems well with your spouse, he must indeed be blessed! You keep on being silent, and you keep on being denied comfort, love, and security. All basic human needs.

PRAYER

Thank you, Lord for your word which is sharper than a two-edged sword. May your word never return void, and may I never use it to get my own way or desires. If someone errs and falls outside of the scriptural guidance, let me remember the times I misunderstood your word when I was young in the faith. Your word is useful for bringing correction, but I understand that not all people want to be corrected, and they wish to remain outside of the guidance within. Please illuminate the scriptures as I dig into them to reveal your will for the lives of your Ishshas, your girls. You alone Jesus are worthy of praise and honour and glory, and I want to glorify your name. In Jesus, Yeshua Ha Mashiac's name. AMEN

Chapter Ten

Pornography

"But fornication and all uncleanness or covetousness let it not be named once among you as becometh saints" (Ephesians 5:3, KJV).

"Mortify therefore your members which are upon the earth, such as fornication, uncleanness, inordinate affection, evil concupiscence and covetousness which is idolatry" (Colossians 3:5, KJV).

The global Christian ministry, Focus on the Family has said; "Many men believe that viewing pornography is, at worst, a private sin with consequences that affect only them. But pornography is in fact a sin that harms the most intimate of relationships — marriage."

TRIGGER WARNING:
Below this sentence is a candid account of a personal experience.

In this scenario, my spouse had stayed up watching TV and I had gone to bed, though not particularly early. I got up to go to the toilet, and I heard the TV. What I heard was him flicking through channels, one minute I'd hear a sound, and the next no sound. The sound I heard made my blood run cold. Suspicions arose, as I knew of this addiction that he was supposedly over, and I crept stealthily down the stairs. I peered around the corner at the lounge ceiling height. What I saw made me want to vomit. He was masturbating, and I could see in the reflections of the glass-fronted pictures on the walls, images of various girls doing the same, and some with men performing sex acts on them.

Even writing that has made me feel nauseous and shaky. I thought after all this time and the heart healing I've been through that I was beyond shockable. Post-Traumatic Stress Disorder (PTSD) is a complex issue, one which I haven't addressed in this book, as I'm no expert. If you can be triggered into a flight/fight/freeze/fawn response by a sound, an object, or a person, you are likely experiencing PTSD. It's ok, you will live through it. It means you are human. You are a flesh being and your flesh body responds. We are also spirit, and when we leave this flesh body at our allotted time in this realm, we will get a new body and a renewed spirit! Meanwhile, we can accept that this is a passing thing, and like all things on earth, it will all be wiped away, along with our tears, fears, and pain. What I've chosen to do is harness those triggers, by aligning with my Father's heart for the lost, the hurting, the prisoner, rejected, captives of injustice that have been normalised in our modern culture. It's time to bring freedom.

I crept back up to the bed, not wanting to confront him–yet. After the initial disgust, as I lay there in bed, I felt utterly rejected. Though I had experienced bad or unwanted sex with him, I still wondered how he could want to watch and do that if he had me. I mean, why does a man need to have frequent regular sex with his wife, and still want that? On a deeper level, how can they do that and say that humans, including those unfortunate girls, are fearfully and wonderfully made in God's image? I mean, how? Those are daughters, girlfriends, and probably wives of men. Someone's daughter, sister, and/or mother–I just didn't get it. I daren't get started on the whole sex industry and the human trafficking that goes on to supply some of these women.

Then, there are the consequences that pornographic habit has on a man, penile erection dysfunction (PED) where they find it increasingly difficult to be turned on enough to have sexual intercourse because the sex they've watched is just insanely

Pornography

impossible to achieve without causing discomfort or pain or inflicting overt male dominance over a passive female. Porn isn't always something that leads to abuse, but you will probably believe it if I told you that it's my belief all abusers use porn. Either in the bedroom with you, or online with others.

If your spouse is using pornography, he is sexually immoral and an adulterer. In fact, adultery in its purest form isn't just about sex, it's about something in your life that is elevated above God. So if God's will and purpose is second place to a person's sexual desires (desire for mastery over others), that is adultery. By the way, it is akin to abandonment. Take for example God speaking through the prophets, when he talks of the nation of Israel being adulterous. He even threatened to divorce himself from his nation! But He didn't, he remembered His covenant!

If you have experienced finding out that your husband uses porn, it is quite likely you have experienced being expected to perform "like a slut," and to enter into the exploration of many and varied versions of sex which leaves you feeling hurt and dirty. Like you want to hide the whole occurrence from God. Would they do it if Jesus was standing there in the room?

When you express your dislike or that these things make you feel degraded and sometimes that it causes discomfort or pain, what is his response? Is he defensive or repentant? Keep in mind that saying sorry isn't repentance, but it can be a start, if it is put right. Is he angry that he got caught or heartbroken over his choices? Does he want to get help? How does he react when you express that he gets help? Does he follow this up?

So we come full circle. How do we confront a man who can be violent, a liar, sneaky, and mentally or emotionally abusive, not to mention financially too!? How do we justify just going straight to the one or two witnesses, without approaching him first? Yet it can be dicey approaching a husband who is unkind, unstable, or predictable. What if they don't believe us? What if we don't get the opportunity to do this? What if our phone calls and texts are screened? Are we watched and tracked? Of course, for multiple hundreds of years, women have been pushed back more and more. In modern times it's gone too far the other way. Where are our strong male role models? Men who want to love and protect. Men who want to provide? Because of this dirge of proper men, we've been left carrying the mantle of the father in single-parent homes. We've carried the mantle of breadwinner or co-breadwinner.

I'm certain this grey area has always existed throughout time, a woman's word against the husband's. Thank the Lord, that Mary the mother of Jesus had a spouse like Joseph, who'd listened to the angelic messenger, and did not give Mary a certificate of divorce. The fact that he was prepared to quietly send her away with a divorce certificate, is in itself a sign that he was a kind man and a godly one. A great example for his son Yeshua to emulate. Women have been taken for a ride long enough! It's time for us to be released from bondage. When we are saved, and we accept Yeshua as our Lord and Saviour, we follow His example and teachings, then we are freed. No longer jew nor gentile, male nor female, slave or free. Just imagine if all the women who were in the body of believers, who are suffering abuse, or have done, were free and accepted, how many more of us could then become an influence to be reckoned with on the world stage? We would take kingdom principles and apply them in the world! Sounds like "as in heaven so on earth," or in a more familiar tongue, "Your kingdom come, Your will be done, on earth as it is in heaven." The apostle Paul writes, "Godly grief produces a repentance that leads to salvation without regret, whereas worldly grief produces death" (2 Corinthians 7:10, ESV)

If your spouse has had issues with pornography, but has repented, sought help, and has stopped using this form of sex, then

Pornography

it is definitely back over to us as to what we do next. Obviously, the Bible tells us to forgive, and so forgive we must—yet. I will expand on this later on in the closing chapters.

God would never abandon you or forsake you. Your spouse may, but God won't. He knows how betrayal feels. He is with you, I can't emphasize this enough.

God loves you! His will is for you to be free; He came to set the captive free! Marriage does not nullify your identity. It should never, ever feel like or be bondage. Once we have a revelation of how much we are loved by God, we are best advised to follow His voice, and His voice has always said "He so loves you, that he sent His only begotten Son, that whosoever believes Him, will not perish, but have life in abundance eternally—my translation! Yes, I've written that three times now—abundant life! Especially within marriage!

"I have loved you with an everlasting love; therefore I have drawn you with loving devotion. Again I will build you, and you will be rebuilt, O Virgin Israel. Again you will take up your tambourines and go out in joyful dancing"
(Jeremiah 31:3b & 4, BSV).

So after that roller coaster of information in this and the previous chapters, you'd be advised to take a break from reading. Not for good, but enough time to reflect on the things that have been exposed so far. Stay with me a while longer, and don't give up on this journey. You have probably been through some of this yourself and if you haven't count yourself as blessed. Help others to become free so they too can be blessed. Blessed and free to carry on in their Kingdom calling. To know God and make Him known.

Can I suggest you write in your journal or make notes on your biggest takeaways, ah-ha moments, or revelations? Wait, you don't have a journal? You always meant to? Start now, it's a good habit to get into!

"Revelation is caught, not taught" –The Finished Life, Pedro Adao

PRAYER

Lord, please help me to not be judge and jury of others. I'm sorry when I've gotten angry and then let anger take control of me. I am a human too, and it is impossible to live without errors occurring. Please forgive me. Lord my body is a temple of your spirit, and so I am sorry when I've treated my own body with indifference, putting into it the wrong foods, and onto it the wrong chemicals. Help me to recognise you in me when I look in the mirror. I am made in your image, bearing your image to the world around me. Thank you that your death and resurrection evidenced an imperishable body to come. I hope, Lord, I can look after this one until that time. Please guide me in this goal. I'm sorry when I've expected things from others that are over and above their own remit. Heal my heart so I can love again. Make me whole and help me to see others as wonderful humans made by your hands.

In Jesus, Yeshua Ha Mashiac's name. AMEN

Chapter Eleven

Coercion

"Death and life are in the power of the tongue" (Proverbs 18:21, NASB).

Wiktionary defines coercion as, "Use of physical or moral force to compel a person to do something, or to abstain from doing something, thereby depriving that person of the exercise of free will."

Let me expand a little on this one. The word of God can be used to compel a person so can deny them their own free will. This is called spiritual abuse. An attempt to exert power and control over someone using religion, faith, or beliefs. Especially when that word is taken out of context, and if the quoted scripture is not tested against the law of grace. The letter of the law kills. The spirit of the law brings life. The spirit of God brings life.

Another way someone can be coerced is if behaviour or emotional responses of the persecutor are guaranteed to get the desired result. Often a person can appear to be pleading with you, momentarily putting the choice in your hands. Or, after you have said no, or I don't want to, they just carry on as if you had said yes, convinced that if they encourage you, or just do it anyway, you will probably enjoy it.

I often-times went out, albeit quietly reluctant, to films or meals feeling wretched: headaches, fever, colds, recovering from cancer surgery. Yet I knew there would be a day or evening alone in the house with a moody husband if I didn't comply. A part of me wanted to be out in the public domain, where he was nice, loving, and friendly. I could even get away with bringing up slightly contentious topics, especially if we were in company. It wasn't that he could be moody when we were alone in the house, though that too, it's that if he 'snapped' he may resort to violence, and I couldn't cope with that. He didn't ever use physical violence on me, he managed to keep his aggression bottled up. Instead, he'd exert sexual domination over me, in the name of passion. He never ever swore in everyday life, not even in extreme circumstances, yet in our bedroom, the filthy words and domineering moves were a type of showing me his strength and alpha maleness.

There was an occasion when he beat up his son because he wouldn't come on a trip with us to visit relatives. He also fought twice with my son, and once pinned my youngest teenage daughter against a wall and shouted right into her face. This incident with his son though, made me feel sick to my stomach. My stepson retreated into himself, refusing to talk; he often did this if his dad was "on one," probably because when he was younger his mum had a violent partner. He displayed "retreating child" just as I had growing up, it was a conditioned response.

I realized if he could do this to his own flesh and blood, he could do it to my children too, which ultimately, he tried on. I felt scared, for myself and them. I'd allowed this man into our lives and home. I'd arrived home to a bleeding, crying teen covered in scratches and bruises, blood on the wall behind him, and a knife embedded in the kitchen floor. The knife had apparently been thrown there by my stepson after he had presumably escaped his father's beating for a moment, or perhaps when his dad had finished, he had resorted to contemplating knifing his dad, or at least threatening to, to get him to stop. His dad fled, leaving the door wide open. Fortunately for his son, who would have had a far worse trauma to overcome had he followed through if his dad remained in the house. I think it was my son who witnessed this, as he'd called me to say "hurry home" because *Marv (my husband) was fighting with *Alister (my stepson). I'd left my shopping on the checkout conveyor belt and drove straight home. The knife upright embedded in the kitchen floor sent adrenaline rushing through me. I was calm on the outside, for the sake of the children, but inside another part of my being went into hiding. I now know this as compartmentalisation. It's a protection pattern. There were so many things surrounding our life with a complex disabled child, and adrenaline was a constant in my life for years. So instead, a bit of me went and hid, whilst the "frontman" continued as if was all in a day's work!

Why didn't I do something about this incident? Fear. That's the simple answer– fear. Escalation and the art of de-escalation is something I've learned throughout my life. My mum had been a single mum, working three jobs all at once. She must have been exhausted. At times she would fly into a rage about something, and during these episodes, I initially spoke belligerently to her, which only ensured the beating continued. Eventually, I learned that if I played the silent compliant card, these outbursts were defused far sooner. I learned that if I cleaned the house, sorted washing, cooked tea, and helped with shopping, she'd be happy. A happy mum meant fewer angry outbursts. I wasn't just doing it for her, I did it for a peaceful life.

More recently, as an adult with three children, married to my first husband, I learnt very quickly that surrender was usually the best option. He was a charmer but had learnt very early on that I was gullible and controllable. It wasn't until years later that I heard an account of a violent altercation between him and his first wife, from the lady next door. One day she'd heard the usual arguing, followed by a loud bang and silence. She thought he'd shot her,

*Names have been changed to protect identity

and so, rather bravely I feel, rushed round, and entered through the open back door. His wife was in a state, with blood on her leg, glass everywhere, and a chair that had broken legs. He'd thrown the chair at his wife, and it hit her in the legs, cutting one deeply, it had also hit the glass door of the oven.

A victim or submitted person is in near total submission to avoid upset if the opposing behaviour is detected. In other words, non-compliance is met with negative responses or actions. So to keep them happy, you go along with it, and try to look as if, and sometimes even partially enjoying the experience. You convince yourself complying is fun, non-compliance will bring a dark shadow into the room. Many years of this "anything for a quiet life" response can erode your sense of self, to the point that you fail to have a strong opinion or desire for anything at all, and simply are there for others. Then when you finally have had enough, people only see the good times, the fun, and the apparent closeness you share with one another. They don't know the behind-the-scenes details.

Eventually, you become sort of accustomed to this way of life, but in your heart, you aren't happy. I used to get comfort from the scripture where the apostle Paul states, "I have learnt to be content in all circumstances" from Philippians 4:11; it's worth remembering, that Paul was referring to beatings, persecution, rejection, and imprisonment.

I simply accepted the status quo. All through my life, I had been groomed by the circumstances in which I found myself, and when I began following Jesus, I took the scripture about winning an unbelieving spouse over by your calmness, kindness, and selflessness. But my second spouse was a born-again, spirit-filled believer so I accepted his behaviour and our weirdly worldly sex life. Then as our circumstances squeezed every ounce of energy from us both, I just accepted his dark moments as par for the course. Gradually, it got worse and worse. The truth of it was,

Coercion

I didn't think I was as important as everyone else. What I wanted, and needed wasn't important. I was way down at the bottom of the priority list. The Bible seemed to confirm that every time I read it. Scriptures like:

- ❖ Do not think more highly of yourself than you ought.
- ❖ Submit to your husband for he is the head of the house.
- ❖ Jesus came, not to be served, but to serve.
- ❖ Spare the rod, spoil the child.
- ❖ Do not stir up trouble.
- ❖ If someone smites you on one cheek, offer him the other.
- ❖ Offer yourselves as a sacrifice, for what you do for them, you do for me.

The list it seemed, was endless!

The thoughts that followed reading those scriptures ultimately came from an underlying orphan spirit which is that God doesn't really care about me, because a dad wouldn't let that happen to his child. Yet on the surface, I was so confident and comforted about God being my Father, always there for me. Unlike my dad who hadn't been, and my stepdad, though he was around, but not really present. All the men in my life had been unavailable, unreliable and/or unstable. And so now, I had this invisible friend, Jesus. In Him, I lived and breathed and had my being. I didn't know real sacrificial love from any humans, but He was my everything. I couldn't see the whole orphan thing until just a short time ago.

It's only as I write this that I realize how long it took me to recognise my circumstances came about because of a deep belief that as a human, I simply just *was*. Things happened to me all the time. But as the veil came away from my eyes, I see now so clearly that until I acted on the revelation that I am a cherished, loved child of God and got the 'hey out of dodge', my circumstances would continue to chase me into a corner! I left Egypt, but it took another year or three to get Egypt out of me! Only now can I cross the

Jordon and enter into the promised land, to enter into my rest. My beloved, you are loved and cherished. As God's child, you are promised freedom from slavery. It's already here. You are free. Now act on that, in humility, stay low, but don't retreat. You've come this far, now just push on through.

Why am I telling you all of this? I hope you can identify with some of my experiences: the grooming, the reluctance to confront, the extenuating circumstances, the misreading or misremembering scriptural quotes and reading the Bible out of context. You see we read it from the backdrop of our lives, applying it to things as they are, but not as things should be. A wounded and trapped animal will try to attack its rescuer. It is merely defending itself from further attack. When God tries to rescue us, we can misread and mishear what He is doing and saying. By doing this we are staying wounded and trapped, or are at risk of losing our life, and sometimes, in extreme cases, our mortal life. Here I'm referring to our spiritual life. The heavenly light in us grows dim, and we can no longer see clearly.

Eventually, a trapped animal can end up just giving up, lying down, and dying. All fight is gone. Why do we give up? Because it appears to us, that God is not on our side. His written word condemns us, even or especially if we leave or divorce. It seems God favours the powerful and appointed significant partner, the man, and tramples the weaker sex– the insignificant woman.

Well, I'm glad I already burst that bubble! And as you read on, you'll see how!

"Never fool yourself into believing that your agenda is sufficiently worthy to somehow justify the manipulation of the people whom you wish to impose it upon."
– Craig D. Lounsbrough: Christian Counsellor and Life Coach

PRAYER

Father God, thank you for loving me unconditionally, and so much that you sent your only begotten son to atone for my sin, and those who sin against me. Thank you that you don't override my free will and that I'm always free to choose to believe you or believe man or the evil voices that try to convince me that I'm worthless. I submit to you because you are holy. Help me to discern with regard to submission to ungodly and worldly demands of others and give me the right words to speak when not comfortable with submitting. Help me to understand your written word so I can apply the wisdom within.

In Jesus, Yeshua Hamashiac's name. AMEN

Chapter Twelve

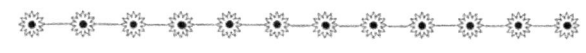

Manipulation

"And it came to pass, when she pressed him daily with her words, and urged him so that his soul was vexed unto death" (Judges 16:16, KJV)

This is a scripture from the account of Samson and Delilah. It demonstrates how, in this case, a woman Delilah, used her wiles to get Samson to relent and tell all! I looked up "womanly wiles", and found an article entitled "Womanly Wiles-When, and When Not to Use Them!" This is what was written: "Seduction, deception, manipulation – men can call it whatever they want, but for me, I consider feminine wiles a powerful art" (Lane). I call it manipulation, and at the height of its use, it's witchcraft. Humans are very good at manipulating. It's a skill that can be necessary to make use of opportunities that present themselves.

As infants, we learn that certain behaviours get satisfactory results, so when we cry, we get food and comfort. Toddlers take this to a whole new level! Take the child who throws a tantrum in a public place to get their own way! It doesn't take long to reap a reward, the ice cream, unless of course, your parents are switched on, and even then, you may not get what you want, but end up getting what you need. For example, reassurance instead of what you thought you needed. In our parental home, we learn how to look as if we're being good when we're not. I used to read at night, under my bed sheets with a torch after I was told to go to sleep!

This can follow us into adulthood where we can be guilty of noticing the bad and not the good. As a teenager, I would notice my mums' faults, and this brought us into conflict. I didn't think it was fair that she smoked and drank alcohol, but I couldn't! I developed an attitude as rebellion crept into my heart. My sense of entitlement grew worse when my friends were allowed out in the evenings, and I wasn't. Bad deeds often scream at us, whereas good deeds are simple, everyday niceties that go unnoticed.

Some adults have grown up with a sense of entitlement, and so have learnt how to use their mood, body language, tone of voice, and behaviour to get out of what they don't want, or to get things they do want. This can come from feeling deprived as a child or being overindulged. In school, we are incentivised by rewards and acknowledgement. On the job, we again look for incentives. Sometimes the place of work uses tactics that are at best unfair, and at worst - abuse. All too often, we end up realizing that our mistakes are noticed, but our great work goes unnoticed.

We can all, at times, feel like we deserve a holiday, a break, and a drink. Although those things in themselves aren't inherently wrong, the emotion behind them can be. Another example would be a scenario when we are refused something, or someone says "No". Sometimes we can decide "No" isn't good enough, and so we wheedle our way around someone until they relent. I'll give you an example I'm horrified to confess; it was I who was the manipulator. In my defence, I would say it's a tool I picked up as a child, and it rekindled within my second marriage. You see when you are seemingly at the mercy of another person's will, desires, and moods, you can become very adept in counter-controlling the scenarios.

I wanted to go up country to visit relatives. In the past, we'd almost come to verbal blows about this, and I anticipated that if I suggested it, he'd say all kinds of negative things that would be possible obstacles and reasons for me not going. I wanted some

Manipulation

time away from him, just a weekend. So instead of "asking if he minded that I go," I framed it another way. I got him into a conversation about his mum who also lived up there. How it's a shame she couldn't come to us like my mum; how much he must miss being able to see her more often "because of our pressing commitments here," and then I walked away and let him mull it over. Sure enough, the next morning he'd come back to me, and suggested that we both go up country to visit his mum and also his aunt and uncle–success! Now all I had to do was agree, which he fully expected, so this made him happy. Then, when he was happy, and therefore benevolent, I suggested I might grab a few hours with my rellies whilst he went to see his aunt and uncle. It was *easy, peezy, lemon squeezy*!

Another scenario is with my cats! Cats absolutely love dry cat food–kibble. They also love being outside at night; however, I don't like them out at night because that's when cats are most likely to meet a horrid end or become injured. So, I don't give them kibble with their meals, or even as a meal. I use it as a "tool" for getting them in. It works even if they've just had a belly full of dinner! It also works to get them out of delivery vans because they're nosey blighters! A shake of the kibble tin is usually enough to bring them running!

I know this second example is far removed from the manipulation discussed here–yet, is it? In an abusive relationship, manipulation is often a tool utilized by both parties. It is the most subtle form of getting what we want, and in some cases avoiding what we don't want. A desired or undesired thing, person, or behaviour. Definitions from Oxford Languages describe it here: "Manipulation is the action of manipulating something skillfully. The action of manipulating someone in a clever or unscrupulous way."

God gave us free will and any time manipulation is present when behaviour from another person uses emotional, mental, and at times physical tactics take away our free will. Manipulation harnesses our emotions to make us feel like there's no other option than to go with it or face the consequences. Satan manipulated scripture to trick Eve. He made it seem as if God was keeping something good from her. According to dictionary.com, manipulation is "The act of manipulating. The state or fact of being manipulated. Skilful or artful management."

CONTROL

I wonder how many times this scripture has been quoted to women over the centuries.

> "The wife does not have authority over her own body but yields it to her husband. In the same way, the husband does not have authority over his own body but yields it to his wife". (1 Corinthians 7:4, NIV)

On closer inspection I have discovered that the word *exousiazei*, which has been written as "have authority over" breaks down as *to exercise or wield power,* so she does not exercise or wield power (over her own body) which doesn't fit, but it also means be ruled or held under authority (from *exousia, control*). It's good to remember that in the original languages of the Bible, scriptures are not usually "the." So could this be translated then as, *the wife should not be ruled or held under authority, her body, in other words, she is not to be controlled,* neither is the husband! One thing is for sure, this verse speaks to me of equality! It's identical for women and men! So, neither is to be controlled by the other!

> "See to it that no one takes you captive through hollow and deceptive philosophy, which depends on human tradition and the elemental spiritual forces of this world rather than on Christ" (Colossians 2:8, NIV).

PRAYER

Lord God, thank you for loving me regardless of my wilful ways. Thank You that if we confess our faults and wrongdoings, and turn away from them, you will not count it against us. I'm sorry Lord for the times I've been manipulative to get my own way, which is witchcraft. I turn from it now. Help me to be honest in my dealings, and not shrink back. I know that when a door shuts, another one opens, and I must learn not to try and get into it through the back door! Lord, help me to forgive those who have manipulated me, either subtly or blatantly. Please lead me not into temptation and deliver me from evil. I trust in you with all my heart and will not lean on my own understanding. Thank you, Lord, for your forgiveness and favour on my life.

In Jesus, Yeshua Ha Mashiac's name. AMEN

Chapter Thirteen

Submit Or Retreat?

"Submit yourselves therefore to God, resist the devil and he will flee from you"

(James 4:7, KJ21)

Submit in today's terms means, "Cease resistance (as to others arguments, demands or control) succumb, surrender, concede, bow, capitulate, yield, budge, relent, acquiesce, defer, quit" (MerriumWebster.Com). This is the opposite to how the Bible writer intended. It was all about working together (Remember *EZER*, which is a word meaning help by opposing, is a word that is also a military term and women have been led to believe it means we are men's helpers!). The opposite, or antonyms include: oppose, confront, object, face, defy, withstand, hold off, combat, counter, repel, thwart, and battle.

So where does that leave us? Well, the Bible is a book that contains so much guidance and wisdom. Do not submit to ungodly spouses, and don't become a chattel who carries out daily tasks that are expected by others. A spouse should help with household tasks too. In the Bible, husbands used to cook, not just wives. Husbands would have had a hand in rearing the children too. You have so much inside of you, and God intends to prosper and not harm you.

In the instance of misplaced submission, there is at best an imbalance of responsibilities, and at worst a harsh taskmaster who is oppressive in word, conduct and deed. This spouse hasn't submitted his desires and actions to God for approval; he is not submitted to God! Even worse is if he feels he has submitted them to God, and has God's blessing, but this leads to action or inaction which is contrary to the law of love, grace, honour, and respect, and when you come into agreement, you are complicit with the works of darkness by default. You are under the influence your spouse is under.

If you are perishing, anxious, feel as if you're disappearing and don't matter, tired all the time, downhearted/broken-hearted, crushed, fearful, hurting, persecuted, hopeless, addicted to coping mechanisms (such as drugs--prescribed or not, alcohol, internet, television, sleep, work), then it's time to incline your ear to His voice, and your eyes to His written word.

> "Trust in the LORD with all your heart and lean not on your own understanding; in all your ways acknowledge Him, and He will make your paths straight. Be not wise in your own eyes; fear the LORD and turn away from evil. This will bring healing to your body and refreshment to your bones"
> (Proverbs 3:5-8, BSB)

Before you go any further take a good slow read of Ephesians 5:1-33 and meditate on it. Take the meaning of it as a whole. What is being conveyed here? That we are to be imitators of Christ.

SUBMISSION BY DEMAND

As you read through this book, I don't want you to feel like you've been an idiot or weak. If you've submitted to the unreasonable and ungodly demands of another, it's because that is what we felt we were to do at the time. Then, gradually you start feeling that perhaps we ought not comply or agree. By then it was an ingrained reaction to just submit. We've all had a skewed understanding of the word because we haven't been taught correctly, or we have but it has been based on a misunderstanding

Submit or Retreat?

of the original intent of the writers, are seeing through a different personal lens or indeed the word just hasn't been translated adequately. Humans have had a long history of complying. Just look at the atrocities carried out in the Second World War, towards the Jews, and more recently, evil stalked in the Ukraine as nightmarish atrocities have been committed. This is and always has been done by soldiers who are complying with orders. The leaders, generals and commanders have blood on their hands, and yet, so do the soldiers. It's just they believe they don't. The problem here is manyfold, not least if they don't comply, news will get around that they are turncoats, and then they are likely to suffer humiliation or even torture and confinement, or even death.

Let's take a look at history. The start of the problem was that humans wanted a person to take responsibility, to be a ruler and arbitrator over them. First, they had tribal leaders, patriarchs, judges, then prophets, until finally, Abraham's tribal offspring got the first recorded earthly king—Saul. This was after being warned it would cost them dearly. It is interesting to note that other people groups had all of these things too, which is evidenced in ancient history and archaeology. God desired to interact with His chosen people, as evidenced both when He met with Abraham in the cleft of the rock *(to protect Abraham from His mighty power and radiance)* and after the exodus from Egypt, in the desert, at Mount Sinai! He spoke and the mountain trembled. The people, in great fear and trembling, sent Moses up to hear for them. The rest, as they say, is history. They crafted a golden calf to bow down before it! Man wanted to be ruled by anybody and anything except for the God of heaven, the creator of the universe. Hierarchical governance was set in motion for God's chosen people. It did not go well.

God's people decided they wanted a human to rule them. Check out 1 Samuel 8:1–18 (ESV) in its entirety, but I highlight some points here:

> Then all the elders of Israel gathered together and came to Samuel at Ramah and said to him, "Behold, you are old and your sons do not walk in your ways. **Now appoint for us a king to judge us like all the nations**." But the thing displeased Samuel when they said, **"Give us a king to judge us."** And Samuel prayed to the Lord. And the Lord said to Samuel, "Obey the voice of the people in all that they say to you, for they have not rejected you, but **they have rejected me from being king over them**. (v. 5-7)
>
> He said, "These will be the ways of **the king who will reign over you**: (v. 11)
>
> And in that day you will cry out because of your king, whom you have chosen for yourselves, but the Lord will not answer you on that day." (v. 18)

Now look at what happens sometime later in the account of King David, when he decided that he wanted intimate relationships with a married woman. Did she have a choice? Not really, he was king! Was she submitted to her absent husband *(He was off at war)*? The consequences of David's sin were visited upon her. Perhaps she was sick with grief at the loss of her husband? Perhaps she became unhappy being taken from her community of friends and family, now living with King David. Ultimately, we'll not know what the cause of her newborn's untimely death was, but she lost her child which must have been painful. It may have felt like God had turned His face from her.

Another example is the stand the Maccabeans made against the sacking and desecration of the second temple which was aided and abetted by Jews who'd submitted to the new Greek authorities.

Submit or Retreat?

They'd fled, forming an army then advanced and stood against the rulers of the day. Because of what they did, a new feast was created, which Jesus attended, the feast is Channukah.

The Sinai sisters who discovered the Sinaitic Gospels disregarded the norm of the time and travelled the world over, often unaccompanied by men! Initially on locating and translating the documents, which centuries before had been dumped by the early monks and got credited to a man because the women were subject to male dominance. The world, it seems, is trying to crush others. Yet God made us all equal. I note that now it has been rightly credited to them–posthumously.

During their lifetime, the University of Cambridge never recognized the sisters for their monumental scriptural find of the Syriac Sinaiticus. But that isn't wholly surprising from a university that denied women full degrees until 1948. Since then, there have been many, many thousands of injustices against people groups, by leaders, both appointed and self-appointed, even or perhaps especially, within Judaism, Christianity, Catholicism, and other God-believing religions, such as in the Muslim, Amish, and Jehovah Witness belief system, where it seems almost universally accepted that women are property and their personal servants/slaves. Modern-day slavery is sadly very real, and not just regarding slave labour and sex and drug trafficking. More tragically injustice, bullying and abuse of ALL types within the marital home have gone so far underground, that though there are a small percentage of awakened believers, on the whole, it is rarely spoken of, much less dealt with lovingly, as Christ modelled.

Someone nominated as head, *(Jesus, husband, parent)* must be submitted to God, through the example of Jesus Christ, Yeshua Ha Mashiach, our saviour, who submitted to God, and to his mum and adopted dad, who were themselves, submitted to God. We are told quite clearly in all the gospels just how they were chosen, and that they chose to submit to Him, and in so doing, the circumstances surrounding her premarital pregnancy. They must have caused a stir in the village, that's for sure! God was always fairly unorthodox and unconventional and Jesus, well, He did what He saw His Father doing!

The word of God also says to submit to one another. So this word is used at times, incorrectly, or rather it is used to serve a purpose, which can be to get a person to be subject to your demands, rather than get a person to come to a place of mutual agreement. That is called discussion. As in, "Come, let us reason together" (Isaiah 1:18).

It has crept in insidiously through all of the church of believers, even sadly into the Evangelical and free church sectors. I can speak of this through direct and indirect experience over twenty-eight years, and more recently through research. Frighteningly, it has been rife within marriages. Furthermore, in recent times the outcry against male injustice and misogyny has tipped the scales too far, in my humble opinion, in a secular society where Feminism, LGBTIQA+, sadomasochism and foetal / infant slaughter are at disturbingly high levels! Meanwhile, women who hold tightly to biblical teaching and guidance from spouses, ill-equipped friends, church leadership, courses, self-help books and misreading scripture, capitulate in all areas of married life *(to sacrifice is to bear fruit)* in the mistaken belief, that as head of the household, the man is "the boss," or in other words is the most important and has the first choice and last word on a matter! Now women are the ones demanding, and it doesn't look pretty.

Submit or Retreat?

It is not wrong to resist unrighteous heads, rulers, and authorities. We were made equal by His blood, just as we were all equal before the fall–male and female humans. "So God created mankind in his own image, in the image of God he created them; male and female he created them" (Genesis 1:27, NIV).

"There is neither Jew nor Greek, slave nor free, male nor female, for you are all one in Christ Jesus" (Galatians 3:28 BSB).

Did Christ always submit to the church leaders; the populace with whom he integrated, and the rulers? Christ and His disciples were an "underground movement," often in hiding and having secret meetings in the dead of the night. Christ often escaped crowds when things got tense. Did He submit to them when they picked up rocks to stone Him? No. He stayed out of the way of trouble when He could, and stayed out of the reach of the corrupt who were under the influence of Rome. He didn't submit to them in our understanding of the word, He challenged them. It was a friend who finally betrayed Him and told the authorities where they were to find Him. He wasn't just blindly accepting their rule. Yes, "render unto Caesar," but here's the thing, if you use the benefits of Roman trade and money, you pay Roman taxes! And if you are in the company of other imitators of Christ, we defer to them, we hear them out–yes? No! We bring words of correction when required and we reason it out. The word translated as submit / subject is *hupotassomai*. It is a military term! If you carry on into chapter 6 of the Bible, he continues speaking in military terms. So in context, the whole thing is using military terms because the audience listening understands military matters. It's like an analogy, a parable.

"Submit to one another out of reverence for Christ" (Ephesians 5:21, NIV).

Ephesians 5:22, "Wives, subject yourselves to your own husbands, as to the Lord" (NASB). The Koine Greek verb υποτασσομαι *(hupotassomai)* is a combination of the verb τασσο *(tasso)* with the prefix υπο *(hupo)*. What we miss right away in English is that this verb was a military term for arranging soldiers in ordered formation to confront an enemy. τασσο could be translated as set, arrange, order, or deploy. Grammar is important too. The ending of the word tells us we're in the passive / middle voice. "Deploy yourself under."

In context, the whole thing is about seeing our unity with each other and with God as a military operation. Talking of leaving behind old ways *(hierarchy)* and continues after by talking about the armour of God as it goes into Ephesians 6. Remember, the chapter numbers were not put in by the writer! The phrase in which the King James Version and some modern translations give submit for the verb *hupotassomai* is embedded within a passage that provides an extended military metaphor. What we're talking about is not an ancient Greek word for abstract obedience but a concrete metaphor of military support.

So then let's look at the flip side, reasoning it out: "Come now, and let us reason together: though your sins be as scarlet, they shall be as white as snow" (Isaiah 1:18, KJV), and for balance: Amos 3:3, "Do two walk together unless they have agreed to do so" (NIV).

So, do we submit or discuss? Do we agree or disagree? After all, we can't agree on everything. Often, we have become so weakened, and our spark of life has dwindled to the point of complete surrender where we capitulate to inappropriate behaviour. Surrender is submission to an overpowering force, person, or situation. I thought to myself more than once, "Well, God will deal with him soon, and then he'll be so sorry!" My spouse wasn't listening to God, (though he was in other areas very adept in hearing God for others) and it took many painful years to come to this understanding. God can influence a person who is submitted to Him, but someone who isn't will push those thoughts away that conflict with his own desires. God will not usually override a person's free will. If that were the case, we would not have the crime and injustice that exists on the earth. It would also mean that Jesus wouldn't have had to die, because God could just rewire us to be perfect again. It's what we pray that is key! If you pray for a way out, it's daft to not see the answer, because God will give us the desires of our hearts, He always gives us a way out. The real problem is that we have accepted the word of god (yes, small "g" because we have made God into a megalomaniac misogynistic taskmaster who created women a little less equal than their human counterparts) as told us by others, in only one or two translations and without further studies into the original message being conveyed. After all, most of the time you don't have any time to do so, right?

As shared in another chapter, my second marriage had other underlying circumstances that meant both me and my spouse were constantly in a state of heightened alert. I lived off adrenaline. Coupled with my previous experience of marriage, and a complicated growing-up phase, I became accustomed to living life on the edge. I had more than one season of taking prescription meds and over-the-counter drugs just to bring sleep on quicker, or even to dampen my senses. Other times, it was alcohol, but the trouble with that is I'd be rendered incapable of driving, from a legal point of view, and also may miss something unless I remained compos mentis. During these dark periods, I felt less loved by God. It was because I felt weak and unworthy lacking in the faith that God could relieve me of these heavy burdens. In this weakened and blinded state, I became submissive to my spouse, dark thoughts, and demons. I had very dark glasses on. The rose-tinted type had left me concluding that those were for dreamers and conjurers! I, however, really saw life for what it was. I all but gave up. Not entirely though. To keep my sanity, or so I thought, I'd just play the game of life, and go where the roll of the dice took me. The roll of the dice is a euphemism for wherever my spouse, health, and child's health took me. So I became a puppet. Swimming against the current is a futile exercise. You become exhausted, eventually giving up and letting the current take you where it will. I was too tired and hacked off to fight. God had my broken and contrite spirit, which apparently, He desires–so that was that. My fate was in His hands – wrong. My destiny is in His hands; my fate is directed by my decisions and those humans I choose to submit to (apart from when I was growing up).

How many times I've felt that God has turned away from me– my cries unheard? Many tears I cried, feeling lost and alone. Why is life so unfair? Up to modern times, we constantly hear of sexual and physical abuse within the home. People are trapped in a cycle of oppression and suppression. Women, children, men, the evil one stalks the earth, seeing how to repress mankind and make them turn from God. Not without success, that is plain to see to believer and unbeliever alike.

What about the case of the Turpin family? The wife went along with the husband, or maybe it may have been the other way, but I suspect not. Those children were kept like slaves, experiencing extreme distress into and beyond adulthood for some. Did they have a choice? Well, it would seem that as they grew older, some began to realise that they had to try and do something that went directly against what their parents told them. But that was after their lives and innocence were taken by those in headship over them. One of the girls broke out of the building and fled for her life. Thankfully, a woman who let her into her home, and then the police officer she called acted on what she was telling them, and they are now free.

We can all suffer tragic and painful consequences of the decisions made on our behalf by those in authority: rulers,

Submit or Retreat?

governments, parents, and husbands. Let me ask you something. If husbands are the head of the house, does that mean they can do anything they want? Does that mean that a wife who is submitted to him cannot do whatever she wants if the husband says so?

One account in the Bible stands out to me, as it demonstrates that standing up for righteousness against or without agreement from those we are supposed to submit to is commendable and rewarded, is that of Abigail in 1 Samuel 25:19-20. Her husband was not respectful of David and his army of men. So Abigail, without her husband's consent, went and delivered provisions to them. She even spoke what could be considered as disrespectful of her husband to David, "And she said unto her servants, Go on before me; behold, I come after you. She told not her husband Nabal. And it was so, as she rode on the ass, that she came down by the covert of the hill, and, behold, David and his men came down against her; and she met them."

Abigail even advised David, despite him being a man and a powerful warrior dressed for battle, and he responded with: "And blessed be thy advice, and blessed be thou, which hast kept me this day from coming to shed blood, and from avenging myself with mine own hand" (1 Samuel 25:33, KJV). Then she went back to her husband who was feasting and drinking. Spoiler alert, it didn't go well for him! "And Abigail came to Nabal; and, behold, he held a feast in his house, like the feast of a king; and Nabal's heart was merry within him, for he was very drunken: wherefore she told him nothing, less or more, until the morning light. But it came to pass in the morning, when the wine was gone out of Nabal, and his wife had told him these things, that his heart died within him, and he became as a stone. And it came to pass about ten days after, that

---

Note: The Turpin case concerns the maltreatment of children and dependent adults by their parents, David and Louise Turpin of Perris, California, U.S. The ages of the thirteen victims ranged from two years old to twenty-nine. On January 14, 2018, one of the children, 17-year-old Jordan Turpin, escaped from the family home and called local police, who then raided the residence and discovered disturbing evidence

the LORD smote Nabal, that he died" (verses 36-38, KJV). Her reward? Well, the future King, and successful warlord David proposed to her! "And when David heard that Nabal was dead, he said, Blessed be the LORD, that hath pleaded the cause of my reproach from the hand of Nabal, and hath kept his servant from evil: for the LORD hath returned the wickedness of Nabal upon his own head. And David sent and communed *(to speak, declare, converse, command, promise)* with Abigail, to take her to him to wife *(אִשָּׁה 'ishshâ)*" (1 Samuel 25:39, KJV).

It's a reminder that during my marriages, I secretly tithed and gave gifts and donations to ministries and charities without my husband's knowledge! I didn't want them to block up our finances by unwise stewardship! But I'm kinda glad the Lord didn't smite them down so I could marry a warlord! (Though I am bride of Yeshua, who is returning in battle mode!)

Agreement/surrender/capitulation can happen through coercion and/or manipulation: the act of coercing; use of force or intimidation to obtain compliance. Not all intimidation is overt, it can be extremely subtle. When you submit your own views, opinions, and desires to a spouse who is not respecting and honouring what you've shared, and who is not submitted to God, there can be a stalemate situation.

> How can we understand that God loves us when, in our marriage, it feels like God has abandoned us?

How can we understand that God loves us, when in our marriage, it feels like God has abandoned us? Because the Bible tells us so: His word, and His spirit. Yet that same Bible also tied me to an unfaithful, controlling spouse. So, God's love was harsh love; love from a distance. I see as I write those words that this was my experience as I grew up with an absent dad and a disregarding stepdad. I was pretty much used to navigating men in my own

Submit or Retreat?

frame of understanding: be kind, don't rock the boat, and bend over backward for any kind of affirmation. Yet I knew that God loved me and hated what was happening to me. It's just the Bible seemed to be imprisoning me, bound for eternity with unfaithful idolaters in a loveless chasm of despair. So if God loves me, the Bible must be misunderstood. It was mainly when I had finally extricated myself from the confinement of the relationship, did I finally started looking for answers. After being exposed to a plethora of fine teachings on YouTube, which as I had surmised, showed me the Bible messages had gotten lost in translation. I also made word studies of the Hebrew language, purely out of interest, and found that Hebrew and Aramaic words and letters have so many different nuances, meanings, and idioms. Koine Greek, which translated from more ancient scripts of the ancient Middle East, also failed to convey, at times, the intent of the original language. In other words, Aramaic to Hebrew to Greek into Latin (initially), English, Russian, German, etc.

Once we have a revelation of how much we are loved by God, we are best advised to follow His voice; and His voice has always said "I love you, I sent My only begotten son, that whosoever believes Me, will not perish, but have life in abundance eternally *(my translation)."* Is your life screaming "abundance?" We are best advised to follow His lead and break the chains of captivity; the prison doors have been flung open, and all you need to do is walk through them. His voice leads you in the other direction away from those things. Especially if those things are happening inside the marriage *(I won't call it the marriage covenant because if those things are present, the covenant has already been broken).*

INACTION IS AGREEMENT

The male is responsible for the harmony in his home, at the same time as being submitted to God. He is not your manager, your parent, or your master—God is. Inaction on our part can look like a place of agreement with the upright thoughts, will, and actions of an unloving, uncaring spouse. My instant thoughts on this are that in a marriage we often believe everything is legally bound together. That submitted means the other is the boss. That is simply untrue because that would mean all other believers are our masters. We would be putting ourselves under the law of the Torah, not the law of grace. Inaction is agreeing with what happens or that what is happening is ok, even when we don't agree in our hearts. No change is needed, yet massive change is needed.

If something is wrong, it needs to be put right. It needs to come before God and be submitted to pastors, leaders, and/or trusted friends which isn't easy to arrange if you are feeling you have to hide most of what you want to bring into the light. Listen to His voice. It is written, "My sheep hear my voice, and I know them, and they follow me" (John 10:27, ESV)

> "Submission is not about authority, and it is not obedience;
> it is all about relationships of love and respect."
> – Wm. Paul Young, Christian Author of *The Shack*

PRAYER

Dear Lord, thank you that as I lean into what you say, I gain discernment and wisdom. Help me to challenge and resist ungodly suggestions. I want to be blessed beyond the curse, and so I choose to bless and not curse. Help me to see who are the people to trust and submit to. To assemble with and form a defence against the enemy, Satan. Lord, I desire to see your Kingdom advancing. By your will being done on earth as in Heaven. I'm sorry for not giving enough time to your word and reading it in my English understanding and context. Lead me to the right Bibles, study tools and discipleship mentors that I can trust. Lead me into righteousness, for your name's sake, so that your name may be glorified in all the Earth. Let me be an example of your grace and favour as I extend what I've learned to others who need to hear the truth.In Jesus, Yeshua Ha Mashiac's name. AMEN

Chapter Fourteen

Signs Of Oppression/Abuse

"Do not conform to the pattern of this world, but be transformed by the renewing of your mind. Then you will be able to test and approve what God's will is--his good, pleasing and perfect will" (Romans 12:2, NIV)

We need to ensure the bride of Christ is not running parallel to societal norms. Our difference should be evidenced as we are counter-cultural within society. Time to renew our minds! In this chapter, I want to share some tips for red flag spotting. If you fall under some of these, your marriage needs help!

SIGNS OF MARITAL ABUSE IN WOMEN IN THE CHURCH

These things on their own are not a sign of abuse, nor if there is an isolated season of errant behaviour. But over an extended period of time, or if many of these things are happening to you, a woman at church, all at once and over a sustained period of time, then it's time to pay attention.

- Can't ever commit to doing something.
- Over committing-doing multiple rotas.
- Sticks with a husband like glue.
- Is hardly ever with her husband when in a group setting.
- Can come out with uncharacteristic statements.
- Quick snipes about the husband.
- Praises husband constantly, celebrating his simplest achievements, or gift as a husband and father on social media.
- Doesn't ever mention her husband.

- Husband doesn't ever come to church even though he's a believer.
- Husband and wife attend different churches.
- She is a quiet, attentive, and diminutive person when with her husband, but a different character if she's alone.
- When a couple makes bad quips or badmouthing one another, making them not enjoyable to be around.
- Doesn't turn up at church with him fairly often.
- Doesn't talk about her own family and friends.
- Stay-at-home mum and homeschooler.
- Only mixes with other couples and not singles.
- Doesn't attend women's events.
- Doesn't attend social events.
- Tells you stuff about her husband that seems unbelievable or out of character for him.
- Husband can fairly regularly seem to go forward for prayer, confess bad deeds, and declare he's working through them.

This list is not exhaustive, and there can be more signs than these. Let me give you an example of how to define if something is abuse or not. We all appreciate that men, especially petrolheads, can at times drive a little too fast for our liking *(not just men but here I'm talking about abuse of women by men)*.

Scenario One

So, Lucy comes up to you after the meeting, and over a coffee, you start talking. She tells you Fred was driving here like an absolute idiot tonight, he almost overshot a red light, and it scared the wotsits out of me. I was so tense, and a little cross with him. So I'm driving home—not him! This is a simple example of a slip of carnality on the husband's part, and not a usual occurrence.

Scenario Two

Lucy comes up to you after the meeting, and you talk over a coffee. She says "Oh, I like to drive, as he always drives like a racing driver. He's so bad. If he drives it causes arguments as I get so nervous, so I drive!" This again doesn't sound great, and it seems he has an incurable habit, but they've worked a way around it that

Signs of Oppression/Abuse

seems to suit both. Now if they had children, then the woman would be right to ask him to be more careful when the children are in the car.

Scenario Three

After service, you're talking over a coffee. Lucy seems a little pale and hardly touches her coffee. Her husband is not far away, talking with your husband. You ask her if she's alright, as she looks tearful. She quietly tells you that he drove here like a madman because she hadn't wanted to come out tonight. Eventually, he insisted, and to show her who was boss he drove badly on purpose to scare her, so next time she'd just come without any hesitation. He's such a nice guy and it seems out of character for him. So you just reply with, "Oh, I'm sure he didn't, he just didn't want to be late."

Keep your ears open, if a woman says something is wrong, then it usually means something's wrong. If she's had the courage to tell you, then that sure says something. Now don't get me wrong, I know some men have been abused by women. But remember 98% of abuse to women, men, or children– is perpetrated by men.

Questions you could ask if you are going to speak with a woman you suspect is being abused/ oppressed are:

- Do you have the freedom to give input on decisions at home?
- What happens when you say "no" to your spouse's requests?
- Do you ever feel fearful around your partner?
- Have you ever been threatened or physically hurt in this relationship?
- Have you ever participated in a sexual act against your will?
- Does your spouse blame you for things that go wrong? How?
- Does your spouse monitor your interactions with friends and family?
- Do you have a say in how your economic resources are used? (Strickland)

As you ask these questions, make sure the spouse in question is not present and ask for detailed examples. *(This is best done in person, as many victims' phones and emails are monitored).*

If you are a counsellor or work in the pastoral team at church, or in a pastoral capacity in your wider community, there are things you need to bear in mind. A woman who has lived in near crisis, or a woman who has been silent or lost her self-respect requires kindness and a patient listening ear. There can be many pitfalls and unwarranted backlash from those in whose company we've been, especially during the crisis years. There are people we've trusted who have misunderstood the degrees of abuse that we've experienced. In some cases, we aren't fully aware of how deep into the cycle we were. After all, an abuser-controller can be quite oblivious to the effects of his behaviour. Often they will have picked up a narcissistic mantle, have had parent issues, or previous failed marriages. Now I'm not saying everyone with a failed marriage is at fault. What I am saying is, most people getting remarried will not put themselves in a bad light, if they've ever talked about the reason the previous marriage failed at all. It took many years into my second marriage before I was told a previous girlfriend threatened to report him for stalking or was going to get a no-contact order if he didn't leave her alone *(I can't remember clearly)*. As our relationship gradually deteriorated, I stayed sometimes in another house, and whilst there I was besieged by him calling, sending messages, and turning up at the door or window or just plain walking right on into the house where I was seeking some peace and quiet. Even when we were together if I was out shopping or visiting my mum, I'd get constant calls and messages! If I was out too long, I'd be read the Riot Act when I got back home. I don't share these to 'vent', but so you can relate.

So, "coming out" can at first seem to bring to mind worse scenarios than putting up and putting out. If you are thinking about revealing just what is going on behind closed doors, or if you leave your spouse without revealing why, your life is about to be put under the microscope. People who you have known for a long

Signs of Oppression/Abuse

time will not understand you leaving if they can't see any reason why. But to protect your own mind and perhaps the errant spouse, you haven't told them fully the real reason. Then there are those who seem to support you both, and perhaps they see your spouse more often than you.

> Within the UK Church community, with almost a fifth (19%) of adults have experienced their partner refusing to accept "No" for an answer.

Ultimately this can lead to some ill advice coming in your direction. Such as warnings to be wise in what you say and to whom—true story! In these times, most of us are conversant with social media, and whilst not pointing any fingers you have a tendency towards the cause of objectified women or over-sexualisation of women, and their plights. You may have joined support groups and may share a post occasionally. Those not "in the know" perhaps wouldn't guess that there's a reason behind your occasional shared posts or rants; after all, there is a cry for help that is other than self-destruction. Whilst we may not be pushed to suicide, or even suicidal thoughts because of our faith, it is such a balancing act to be heard without pointing the finger. It is merely a natural reaction to being silenced, and often for years.

Remember the figures from Premier Christianity: Domestic violence is prevalent within the UK Church community, with almost a fifth (19%) of adults experiencing their partner refusing to accept "no" for an answer when he or she wants to have sex. According to an exclusive survey conducted by *Christianity* magazine, for 6% of the 443 people who completed the survey, which was held in conjunction with domestic abuse charity Restored as part of their "In Churches Too" campaign, this is a frequent experience.

If a person is suppressing their own thoughts, words, and actions in favour of another, that is a sign they are being oppressed. Again, in this instance, I mean constantly suppressing their own desires, not the occasional biting of the tongue.

PRAYER

Lord God, thank you that You never will leave me nor forsake me. I'm sorry for the times I have believed that You have. You made and make me brave, because it says in Your word that You did not give me a spirit of fear. Please forgive me for shrinking back and being a coward. This has allowed the enemy a foothold into my life and has perpetuated my spouse's journey towards ungodliness. I've misunderstood Your heart and Your written word. From this day, I will study Your word to become wiser in Your ways. I want to do what I see You doing, which is releasing captives from bondage, starting with me.

Please bring to mind any unlawful and unhelpful mindsets and beliefs that oppose You. Anything that opposes Your mandate, which is to see heaven on earth, to take dominion over all unsound doctrines, the doctrines of demons. Anything which opposes personal freedom is a doctrine of demons. I am a bondservant of Jesus, Yeshua, I am Your daughter, and You are God of all the heavens, and I am a citizen of heaven, by rights, through the blood of Jesus, through adoption. I am seated in Heavenly place in Christ Jesus! Please heal me of any disease and sickness, including those that come from a heart deferred, stress, anxiety, and fear. Please help me to worship You fully, in spirit and in truth, because when I worship You, my strength will be renewed, and I will become strong and rise up on wings, just as an eagle does!

In Jesus Yeshua Ha Mashiac's name. AMEN

"The most common way people give up their power is by thinking they don't have any."
– Alice Walker, Author of The Color Purple

Chapter Fifteen

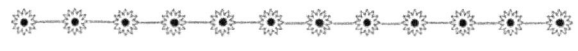

Hide And Seek

"Everyone who does evil hates the light, and will not come into the light for fear that their deeds will be exposed" (John 3:20, NIV).

THE PROBLEM

Western civilisation is counter-patriarchal. Though there is a hidden agenda which you can find if you just scratch away the surface. Then, there's the Middle East and Asia which are unashamedly patriarchal.

In some cultures, however, there is a matriarchal system: usually African and some Brazilian cultures. These societies do not scream equality, women's liberation, or even feminism, but rather, it is a subtle acceptance of the natural order of things. To me, it makes so much sense, because older women are the mothers and grandmothers. It is they who instil security and respect. It is they who nurture and shape the generations after them. It is they who teach their sons, daughters, nieces, nephews, and grandchildren. These societies have fairly strict moral codes; perhaps some are different and even appear immoral to outsiders. Generally, though, they are not viewed quite as liberal as ours.

In the West, our liberal views, plus the complete break away from the accountability structure that is community seem to be core deep within faith structures and in the world. Spread out into sprawling towns and cities focused on earning enough to cover the cost of having all that glitters because, "we're worth it" has left us bereft of the moral compass that comes with mutual responsibility; until the extra costs come piling in: housing, transport, fuel and taxes. So many of us get pulled into this dichotomy; what we desire is more important and takes priority over what we need. Duty unto others is a byword; do unto others as you would have done to you has little meaning where there is no self-respect nor acceptance that the human body should be treated with respect.

Meanwhile, as people of faith, I feel we've taken our eye off the ball: to know God and make him known. How can we do that if God is not in every detail, of our life, our actions, and our choices? Our patriarch is Father God, and we are entrusted to our earthly father's care as infants until we're married! But that's where it all started to go terribly wrong!

Despite this, as women of God, we have a responsibility to model and teach those who are younger what is good, kind, and right. Even if we've not had a good role model as a dad, everyone has a basic knowledge of what is good, and what isn't. It becomes even more challenging if we marry unwisely. We can hardly do that effectively while submitting to the unreasonable immoral and unkind acts of a spouse who won't submit to God, nor anyone else. Sadly, it also models to the children that this behaviour is acceptable, reasonable, and right. And so, we create a generation of confused self-centred orphan-minded adults, mixed with hormones and a culture that allows anything and everything gives us a witch's brew of anarchy. Resentment and unvented frustration are a powerful brew. Why has it taken so long to realise this?

Men of God, you have been given the responsibility of bringing harmony into your homes, and also for speaking out for those in bondage, poverty, the widow, and the orphan. It seems more like these things are actually created by fallen-away men who worship:

er, self-image, celebrities, and the sexualisation of women. By worship, I mean the concept that these things become more important than living as a believing Christian.

So what can we do to stop the cycle?

HIDDEN

The results of hiddenness are usually devastating. This is probably due to the fact that men don't talk about such things with their peers, especially at church, and they certainly won't admit that they have issues. Perhaps it's because they believe there are no issues?

> *"But if they had stood in my council, they would have proclaimed my words to my people and would have turned them from their evil ways and from their evil deeds" (Jeremiah 23:22, NIV).*

Women likewise can hide what's going on to protect themselves, and an errant spouse or be in denial. If a woman is gradually isolated away from friends and church members, she can remain hidden. This can happen organically through the woman simply having no time to attend. Not to even mention that whilst it may not be an occurrence at present, there will undoubtedly be those who have endured this abuse in the past, and they are unlikely to talk about it. Some women end up church hopping, whilst others just stop attending. In this way, they remain hidden in plain sight.

How can we help women if they haven't revealed themselves?

There are many ways to flush us out! There are a variety of ways to ensure that no stone is left unturned in our desire to create a safe environment where ALL members of a church can be at least seen if not heard, feel safe and most importantly be led into the freedom that Christ bought for them. There is no way that a church that looks outward into the wider community can fail to look first into the current church membership; by a member here, I don't mean the clerical, made an oath, fully subscribed member of an institution or denomination. I mean, a regular attendee, or a person that has attended sporadically for many years *(I was that person!)*.

> If a woman is gradually isolated away from friends and church members, she can remain hidden.

There should be a women's ministry with leaders who are trained in looking for signs of abuse. There should be training offered to church members, to raise awareness. There could be a mixed Bible study aimed at bringing balance to marriages. This could be online. There could be notices in the lady's toilets, to raise awareness of abuse, and raise awareness of support for those who could feel they are abused. There should be a contact number.

Remember not all who are abused can identify that this is the case; be vigilant and alert. There are times I've seen behaviour that leads me to believe that there is an imbalance of power going on. In most cases, the family is the sort who is just passing through. f things get uncomfortable for the husband who feels he is the ultimate authority and wives should be in submission or subordinated, and there is teaching that is contrary to this; they will move on. Often these are the sort that joins or starts a house church, Bible study group or home group. This can be so the man can assert his authority by bringing and discussing scriptures that suit his misplaced beliefs, and/or surrounding himself with like-minded individuals.

Remember, women who are being controlled often have their conversations monitored. So no obvious messages should be sent, or left on personal phones or computers (emails), victims are often unable to attend church regularly or attend midweek sessions.

An idea would be to offer support to mother and toddler groups, sewing or craft groups, one-day or half-day events, and during the week instead of weekends. Don't advertise to the whole church what the talk is, just bring it to the group as a conversation. This doesn't just need to be aimed at believers either. Plenty of unchurched, pre-believers also suffer domestic abuse. In fact, statistically, they are more likely to recognise and/or reveal their situation than believers! In society as a whole, low-key abuse is recognised and even accepted by the status quo. Where do you think sayings like "better the devil you know, than the devil you don't know" come from?

In her book entitled, *Is It Abuse,* Darby A. Strickland wrote: "The conflict between the will to deny horrible events and the will to proclaim them aloud is the central dialectic of psychological trauma. People who have survived atrocities often tell their stories in a highly emotional, contradictory, and fragmented manner which undermines their credibility and thereby serves the twin imperatives of truth-telling and secrecy. When the truth is finally recognised, survivors can begin their recovery."

In this particular arena, there has usually been no specific training or previous experience. However, this does not mean we can just bypass the uncomfortableness by avoiding such conversations. Jesus gave an ear to those who spoke to Him, even and more often to strangers. How much more should we be there for our sisters in Christ who are often themselves new to the whole spilling the beans thing? What is vital is that this doesn't get into the wrong hands and become gossip. The best case scenario is that you ask if it's ok to go to a person who has the responsibility of pastoring for accountability, or better still that the person has a friend present, or you do.

With this in mind, it is wise to allow the person who says they've been, or are being oppressed, room to speak. Even if you are feeling ill-equipped to listen, it is important that the person feels they can trust you, and it is okay to feel uncomfortable. Giving them the opportunity to at least vent whilst at the same time reassuring them that it's ok is better than them being locked into a vacuum of silence.

Sometimes you'll hear that these women have been to counselling, both alone and as a couple. This can sometimes leave them feeling even more isolated, as they are unwilling to spill the beans in case they are told, yet again, to be kind to the husband, or speak with the husband and discuss issues. In cases of oppression *(which is also known as abuse)* a husband is unlikely to respond favourably, if at all, to a spouse he sees as his property for all intents and purposes. The two are one, therefore her body is his body, and he can do what he likes because; wait for it, the Bible tells him so. Another thing to consider is that though it seems as if the husband is going to these sessions, it can be of no help if he makes no real and lasting changes. Ultimately, if he appears to be willing to fix the problems it sows false hope in the heart of the wife, who stays in the cycle longer. It's all part of the control game. An abuser doesn't necessarily want to destroy the victim, just bring them to heel. A bit like any infestation of pests that don't kill the host or they themselves will then die; locusts eat everything green then have nothing left to eat, so they die. In the same way, an abuser, who has an over-inflated perception of entitlement, lives off of the benevolence of the host. So to a degree, they must ensure the host has some respite before launching a new assault. The constant see-saw merry-go-round existence will keep playing out until one person leaves the cycle.

Just over half of respondents who had suffered domestic violence had sought information or help. Friends were the first people that victims had sought help from, closely followed by the church. However, only 42% agreed with the statement: My church is a safe place for people suffering abuse and 40% were unsure of whom to contact in their church if they, or someone they knew, were suffering domestic abuse. Sexual assault or forced sex occurs in 40-45% of marriage relationships, marital rape occurs in 10-14% of all marriages as seen by the previous figures from the States, Focus on the Family, and in an article by Darby Strickland on Sept 13th, 2021.

So how can we help?

Years ago, when I was accessing a counselling service, I was informed of the Rescuer, Persecutor, Victim triangle. The psychotherapist explained this to me with a diagram; it was an inverted *(or upside-down)* triangle. It's a cycle that abusers and manipulators often fall into a habit of adopting.

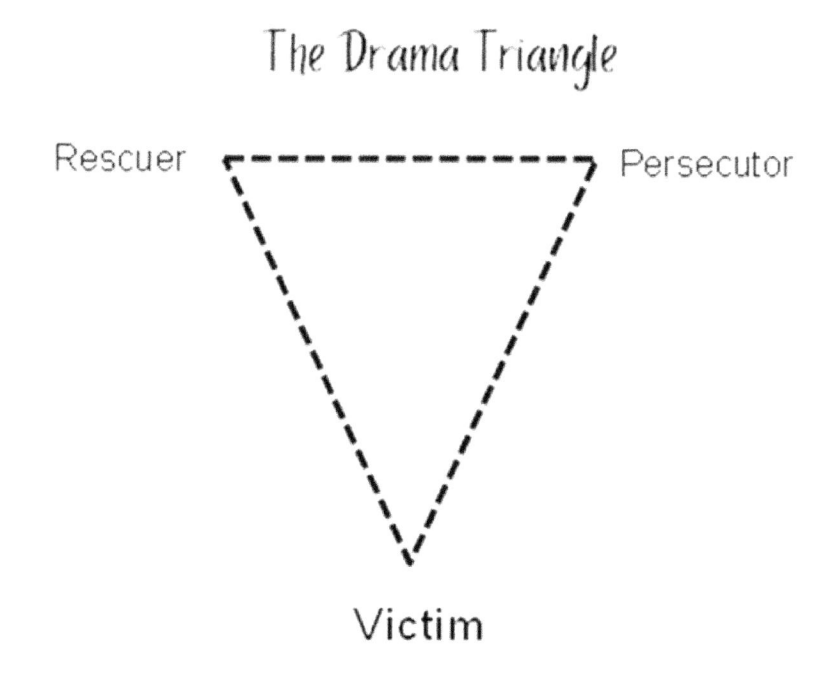

The Drama Triangle

Rescuer — — — — — — — — — — → Persecutor

Victim

The Rescuer:

In this mode, the person doesn't recognise the other person's capacity to help themselves. Basically, the person would soothe the victim. The rescuer needs to feel important. This is classic enabling behaviour. This ensures the victim stays in victim status, and the rescuer takes attention off of their own issues, where the main point is to avoid confronting them.

Signs of the rescuer:
> appear self-sacrificing
> overly helpful and facilitative
> like to be needed
> prone to meddling unnecessarily
> engulfing

The Persecutor:

In this mode, the person doesn't respect other person's views or integrity: critical, controlling, oppressive and blaming others/the other person. They are angry, authoritarian, enforce rules and are superior. They keep the victim *oppressed* by threats and bullying. The persecutor usually presents when building resentment by the other whilst they are in rescuing mode is being unappreciated or finding victimhood too oppressive.

Signs of the persecutor:
> angry, openly or passively
> aggressive
> judgmental
> bullying
> demanding
> spiteful and scornful

The Victim:

In this mode, the person doesn't value self and defers to others. The victim plays poor little me, feeling powerless, hopeless, ashamed, and helpless, with poor problem-solving and decision-making skills. This person has poor insight, cannot feel pleasure in life, and feels like persecutors are everywhere. They need a rescuer to save everything, but it never changes anything

> manipulative
> poor me syndrome
> helpless and needy
> complaining and whining
> fretful
> downtrodden
> blaming others

Now all three roles can be played by an abuser-oppressor, but the interplay between this and a person on the receiving end can get complex because depending on which mode the abuser-oppressor is in, the other person can end up appearing to adopt one of the other personas as a reactionary response. In an unbalanced marriage, sometimes a person who is being repressed, oppressed, or treated with violence, can and will have outbursts of retaliation. So where we have learnt to give in, give up, or face the consequences, at times something may snap, and we retaliate. This gives an abuser an opportunity to challenge your behaviour and your godliness.

This is in part due to another triangle that I have learned: The Parent, Adult, Child triangle *(there is the retreating child and the rebellious child)*. In this triangle, there is an interplay of roles; each adapting in response to the attitude adopted by the other.

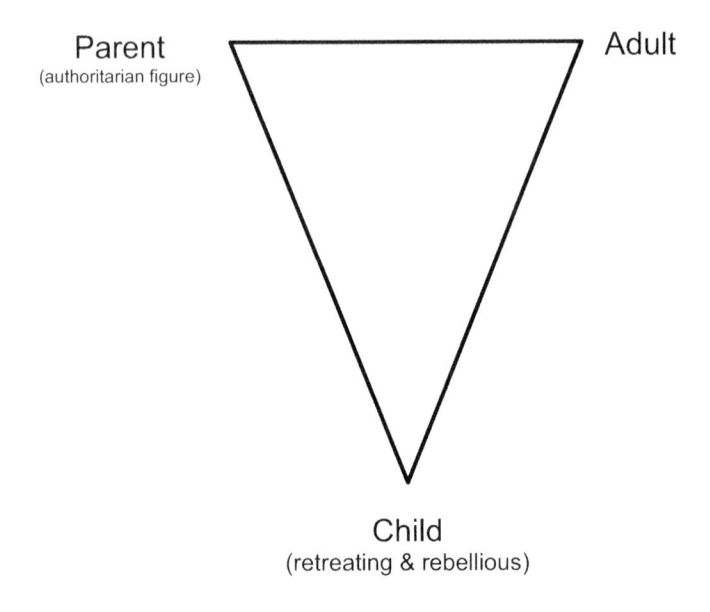

```
      Parent                          Adult
(authoritarian figure)

                    Child
            (retreating & rebellious)
```

Think of a parent being an authoritarian figure. A child has to comply and do as they're told. Compliance is different from retreating. A retreating child responds in this way due to fear or mistrust of a parent. A child who manipulates can do so to get their own way, either out of fear or out of opportunity, because of an imbalance in the home: such as a parent who doesn't inspire respect through their behaviour–the "do as I say not as I do" model.

An adult doesn't need to show authority to another adult (except in the wider societal norms of the public: police, government officials, or rank within the police/armed forces) A lot of marriages suffer and flounder due to this one. You see both spouses have to stay in adult mode, in which case there is a balance of responsibility. However, if one adopts another role, such as "the parent," then it becomes unbalanced. Think of the parent-authoritarian role being akin to the "'rescuer." The other will then adopt an attitude of the "retreating child (victim) or that of the "rebellious child" (persecutor). A retreating child then becomes a victim of control. The rebellious child often gets the brunt of anger, and arguments as fights ensue. In a different scenario, a victim of abuse will at times rise to the bait and adopt an attitude of anger and indignation: adopting the parent, and this time persecutor! The true oppressor can then default to "victim/retreating child," and in so doing become quite manipulative towards the actual victim who is being oppressed.

Through this, the other triangle can come into play: the persecutor-rescuer-victim. It can be interchangeable during a heated exchange, and in worst-case scenarios, an abuser will ultimately take the upper hand: through sanctions, sulking or violence. Sometimes there can be a kiss and makeup session; followed by a night of passionate sex, whereupon an abuser can often exert his power over a wife who doesn't realise she is being conquered in bed. I have suffered this type of assertive dominance during sex. It's usually not until afterwards that I realise the events prior have led to the unusual show of aggression and a level of subjugation during sex. Quite frankly, it felt a little like I had been a retreating obedient child to a dominating parent. I had been subdued, conquered, and shown who is boss. Then, there he lies in a deep and satisfied sleep; whilst I cling to the edge of the bed and weep, feeling violated and unclean. It didn't help that my husband enjoyed playing out sexual acts portrayed on pornography channels and online videos. As I write this, I wonder, as I have before, whether some enactments were with underaged girls and boys who were portrayed as naughty children who need to be disciplined through derogatory sex acts; the thought sends icy shivers through me.

Now, I'm not saying everyone needs to undergo counselling or psychology training! What I would suggest is that in any church that has a children's team that undergoes training, equal training ought to be given to volunteers who wish to be good stewards of the adult population. On another level, it would be wise to let all members realise the importance of being on the lookout for signs of oppression, abuse, or predation.

I say this last one, predation because of my direct experience in two gatherings; One is historical, in that I attended a small church from 2003 until I was forced to leave. The reason was that not one, not two, but three men insisted on pursuing me; trying to have conversations, inappropriate familiarity, and downright blatant flirting– oh and of course, the "greeting your brother and sisters with a kiss." It even continued after I got married! I stopped attending after asking the church leader to talk with them all, which he did, but it didn't stop. One was a twice married and divorced single. There was alleged abuse in his previous marriage: one was an abusive alcoholic according to his wife (open knowledge at that time), and one was a reformed ex-convict who'd married an underage girl at Gretna Green many years prior, but she'd gotten ill and died prior to his prison sentence. After about two or three years, I returned there with my husband, but these men were still trying to get close to me, so we left.

Now up to date, having been separated from my husband for seven years, I've recently been attending a twice-monthly worship event, along with a friend of mine. On one occasion a man introduced himself to me and we began talking, which seemed harmless enough; he shared he was divorced, and I said I was separated pending divorce, among other things. A bit later, he came back and said he had a scripture for me. It was one of the scriptures warning people not to divorce but instead try reconciliation. I said to myself, "Oh, yeah," a word from God–huh? It was: 1 Corinthians 7:10-11, "To the married, I give this command (not I, but the Lord): A wife must not separate from her husband. But if she does, she must remain unmarried or else be reconciled

Hide and Seek

to her husband" (NIV). That was enough for me, I finished the conversation as fast as possible and shortly after when we were driving home, my friend told me that years ago he attended her church with his wife. That there was something hush-hush going on and it resulted in divorce. Furthermore, two months later, there he was again, homing in on me! I didn't engage with him for long and chose to excuse myself to talk to someone else. Later as I was worshipping and dancing with my flags, I got hit by the awesome presence of the weightiness of God, and was bent over facing forward, flags now dropped to the floor. It was during this very holy moment that said man was suddenly by my side, put his hands on my back to let me know he had something to say and started talking. It was wholly inappropriate on two levels: both spiritually and as a man to a woman, he's not in a relationship with. It broke the moment. Again, in the car, on the drive home, I spoke to my friend about it. She revealed he'd also put his hands on her too. This man is a predator.

The reason I share this is because, if we are regulars, or long-term irregulars (like me), and you know who's who and what's occurring in the building, you must have an awareness of the plausibility of occurrences like these. I'm surely not the only one who's been stalked at church. Another single lady, whom I know from the same church has experienced this subtle harassment both in and out of the building. Folks, we must keep our eyes open and protect the women as well as the children. It is hard for many of us, within the church environment, to give a man the brush off in a firm but kind way. So often, the men don't feel anything untoward has happened. It can make women leave, she may not find another church, so, she may slide in her faith.

Women must be equipped to deal with these situations. We have no escorts these days, in fact, the word is now misappropriated to mean a "lady friend," often a paid one, who can go further than just escorting functions! Perhaps I ought to use the really old-fashioned word–chaperone.

> "For evil to flourish, it only requires good men to do nothing."
> — Simon Wiesenthal, Holocaust Survivor, *The Sunflower*

PRAYER

Dear Lord God, you made us in your image, male and female you made us. In a marriage, a mystical union occurs, one that mere humans cannot sometimes fathom. It is a message to your people, whom you now call BRIDE. There are so many hurting and lonely people Lord, who want a companion, but the truth is we need to look to you first, and then our hopes may come to pass. I want to be your voice, your hands, and your eyes, and like almost every human, I want to be loved. The love I've been shown has at times not been good love, but instead warped and twisted and worldly. I forgive those people now *(name them here as you feel led)*. I also repent for times I've not demonstrated love to others and turn back towards you and away from wrongdoing. Please help me to see the truth in others, and to recognise the weaknesses in my own character. Lord, please reveal any iniquity within me that may be causing the way people perceive me to be blurred or skewed. Help me to recognise things in others which may need addressing, and to be bold and speak to church leadership or to the person directly. Lord, I ask for favour as I begin a dialogue with those with ears to hear, regarding inappropriate behaviour, and controlling others whom we are meant to respect.

In Jesus, Yeshua Ha Mashiac's name. AMEN

Chapter Sixteen

Who Am I?

"Do you not know that your bodies are a temple of the Holy Spirit who is in you, whom you have received from God? You are not your own"
(1 Corinthians 6:19, NIV).

Have you ever heard the expression; we were made to be helpers– ezers? That a woman's role is to enable. I have, many times over many years! It helped form a desire in me, to fulfil that role to the utmost within my marriage. There was a problem with this, according to my husband's actions, I fell short. This caused me to feel like I was unappreciated, and no matter what I did, I wasn't as great as the head of the house. However, *ezer* does not apply to a woman, wife, or female! It is not a title, purpose, or role. It is a function. Moreover, it is a soldier function– a warrior!

The word, *ezer* or helper shows up: Twenty-one times in the Old Testament. Twice to describe a creature to help the man *(Genesis 2:18 & Genesis 2:20)* Once to explain that the Hebrew people would not be considered a help to Egypt (Isaiah 30:5). Once to explain how the Prince of Jerusalem would be removed, taken to Babylon, and his helpers scattered to the wind (Ezekiel 12:14) ***All other times helper was used as a descriptor of GOD.***

The word *ezer* is used throughout the Bible, not referring just primarily to women, but to men, nations, God and even armies! The word *ezer* is an action. Even more, the action of a brave soldier and God himself! This word is found 22 times in the Bible, and only twice is it referring to the companion that God intended for His lonely man who needed another person that he could interact with intimately. Not only that but directly after saying "I'll make an *ezer* for him," God made all the animals! But, (from amongst the animals) no suitable helper, *ezer* was found!

Earlier in Genesis 1:27, *neqêbâh* is the word used for female, but it is also used for a female child and female animal. The word for male is also the same for humans and animals!

A woman is not her reproductive assignment, which is a function, nor her readiness to assist which is a role. Her identity uttered from the male's mouth from the outset was a wife; complimentary to the husband: equal to or even a part of, partner, or other half. I have often struggled with the word *ezer* because I always felt a slight injustice. I felt that women are supposed to be more, so much more than just a support or help meet for the man. It denotes far more than a mere assistant! It more accurately describes a strong, knowledgeable, experienced ever-ready help in times of trouble: a warrior, powerful, fierce, and up to the task! Now, let me introduce you to *ISHSHA*!

I-SH-SH-A in Hebrew is written and read right to left so *a-sh-sh-i*.

Hebrew words are so much more than simply a word! The letters each have words, numbers, and meanings; the combination of which gives a full definition of the word. Pronounced *eesha*. The *HEY/HET* is silent so it should be pronounced the same as in *it* or *ee*(ie) as in thief. **alef** (a) **shin** (sh) **shin** (sh) **hey** (I) reversed to our left to right I-sh-a.

Who Am I?

Aleph	**Shin**	**Hey/Het**
Symbol is OX which means beginning.	Symbol is teeth/crown	Symbol is a homemaker in the tent
Value = 1 as in first (oneness of God)	Value = 21	Value = 8
Meaning is master, teacher and wondrous	Meaning tooth, steadfast, change, return and year	Meaning is to be disturbed and behold

I love that wife is, a oneness of God (in His image), steadfast, can crush and destroy an enemy, or be crushed (or *crusher) or crowned depending on how she is valued. ISHSHA is here to wondrously behold. In the home, she is royalty and comes first if it's a happy marriage!

Ishsha is the name the male gave to the female human that was to be his equal, a worthy companion for the male. Formed not from the dust but drawn forth using DNA from him, who himself carried the DNA and image of God; drawn forth from him, by the loving careful hands of their Creator-Father!

So girls, ladies, embrace your inner Eesha!

In Genesis 2:23, the first word Adam purportedly spoke was Eesha. Unless he spoke to the animals, though one could argue they spoke with a serpent, and later on in the Bible, a donkey spoke to a human! To be honest, I've often believed, particularly now, I have a deeper cultural and linguistically nuanced view of the very ancient middle east, that the writer, some thousands of years after the event (the first humans lived into their 700s for quite a while), when referring to the serpent, was not meaning a snake by physical appearance, but to the portrayal of a slippery character who speaks with a forked tongue. We also need to accept that this account was written retrospectively, way after the fall, where the deceiver had been cursed to crawl on the ground, like a snake.

*Remember that Eve's offspring was going to crush the serpent's head? Genesis 3:15

We know that Lucifer was a fallen archangel, beautiful to behold, but dangerously persuasive. He coerced and maneuvered a third of the heavenly host to join him in his refusal to submit to God, His creator *(Something we need to remember when considering spouses who no longer submit to God!)*.

So eesha is the word the male used to describe her and to identify with her! He wasn't referring to her gender! This word is specific to "wife." He was saying, wow, she's like me, she is me all over! We could even surmise that in the absence of mirrors, this was the Stone Age, he didn't know what his own image was in totality. Imagine looking deeply into another person's eyes, the window to the soul, for the first time! In Genesis chapter one, it does record that there were male and female beings or *adamahs* made in the image of God! They were to multiply!

So, back to the male. He might have said, she came from me, she is not me, but she is just like me; but wait, there are some differences! She's more delicate, wow, she's gorgeous, two are better than one. Let's go and get this wilderness sorted and bring it back to order–let's do this! Together we're stronger than one!

Later, after the fall, the writer of Genesis names them Adam *(from the earth)*, and Eve *(mother of all living)*. We must remember, this was all in the Mesolithic Period *(middle of the Stone Age)*, and for hundreds and thousands of years, the story was verbally passed on from generation to generation. The Bible is a literary work from the memory and oral passing down of history through generations, so we can veer too far down a bunny trail by attaching literal significance to specific words. Adam and Eve may not have understood, nor required proper names in our understanding, and beings were often known by their appearance, occupation, character, or where they were from.

Who Am I?

> Applying Mitochondria DNA and archaeological evidence integrated with Judeo-Christian and Muslim Scriptures, I show that after God created Homo sapiens, He created the Biblical Adam and Eve circa 9,700 years ago, and that Adam and Eve were the prototypes for present-day man, referred to in my paper as Homo sapiens -- very wise man. Moreover, archaeological evidence suggests that Eve and Adam were created during the Mesolithic Period and co-existed with Homo sapiens and that Homo sapiens were subsequently eliminated. Thus, all humans today are descended from Eve. (Choice)

There have been disputes over the centuries by people who have conducted research and even rabbis from many years ago, who cannot agree if the word *ish* and *isha* have different root meanings, or if they are the same. Suffice it to say, the fact that we're not solely an *ezer:* though that transpired to be more powerful than I initially perceived when fully comprehended is powerful enough. I was a happy girl when I discovered we are MORE THAN what we can offer, our role or our purpose. God desired offspring on the earth, and we were the vessels through whom this would occur! We were set apart, chosen and to be cherished; a perfect team, as one, requires the other.

Males are physiologically different because they are to protect. This is to ensure that God's earth offspring, and the offspring carriers *(females)*, who carry His likeness and glory spread out, subdue, and overwhelm corruption, by submitting to God. That we have equality that we're on equal standing in God's eyes. We are all equal under one God, and to earn a place as the head of a household, in the way that Jesus is head of the church; the *Ish*-husband has to be Christ-like, obedient to God, submissive, servant-hearted, self-sacrificing and lead by example. They must not exert pressure, use confusion, twist scripture, gaslight and use otherworldly leadership/boss methods. Now, I'm not talking about perfection here, all marriages have areas where there are slip-ups and disagreements: things that need putting right with discussion and coming together. However, if continued, ill-treatment leads to the detriment of your happiness, something is seriously amiss.

Here's an interesting thought; the woman was made from the rib of a red earth man, *adamah*. Ribs are meant as a covering of all the vital organs, like a protective shield. Have you ever felt that you have to shield or protect your spouse? I can guess the answer! Here is a more pertinent question; have you felt you needed protection from your spouse?

I encourage you to read these scriptures in your Bible, they are enlightening, encouraging, and edifying! Cross-referencing scriptures quoted in a book is a brilliant way of making something stick. You are more likely to catch the intent of both the author of the book in your hands, but also the original author who wrote the scripture. Remember, the Bible is God-breathed, His spirit was in the human that noted those details, and in the human, the scribe (this was usually the case).

Genesis 16:1, 2
Proverbs 31:10-31
Judges 4:4, 5
Number 27:1-7
Esther 1:10-12, 4:15-5:3

Note if the meaning seems different in some versions. Write any thoughts that may have come up.

Read back to what you've written and seek God asking what He wants to highlight for you.

It was common to offer services as a writer in biblical times, as not many people could actually write. It would have meant the end of the oral-only tradition, as scribes sat with a person dictating what to write–secretaries of the ancient world. Yes, there were ghostwriters way back in biblical times–Holy Ghostwriters!

> *"When a wife has a good husband, it is easily seen on her face."*
> *– Johann Wolfgang von Goethe*

PRAYER

Father God, please hear me as I call You, my Daddy. I am Your child, I carry the heavenly DNA imparted to me as I accepted Jesus, Yeshua Ha Mashiach into my heart and soul. You are a good Father, far better than any father on the earth. I am blessed beyond the curse. Your promises to me will endure. Please help me to fully comprehend just how much You love me. Nothing can separate me from Your love. You have never left me, nor forsaken me. You have witnessed my whole life so far, from the inside of me. Any misguided action perpetrated, or word spoken to me was also done to You. I'm sorry for the times where in apathy or fear I didn't resist or gently rebuke the perpetrator. I forgive (*insert name here and repeat this part for every individual that needs forgiveness, including yourself*). Please help me to move past this so I can have more clarity in my life. Please level out the terrain I have ahead of me. When I forgive others, You forgive me.

In Jesus, Yeshua Ha Mashiac's name. AMEN

Chapter Seventeen

God's Favoured Women

"Coming in he (Gabriel) said to her 'greetings favoured one, the Lord is with you'" (Luke 1:28, NASB)

Here are some women of the Bible with whom you may, or may not, yet be acquainted. This is just a small portion of them. What I'd like you to know is that God is no respecter of persons. In other words, He's impartial. His spirit and favour were on women as well as men. It was all down to the woman, her faith, her understanding of God, and in some cases, the Mosaic laws! These women were smart and wise. They were not afraid to go against societal norms if they felt God leading them that way.

Anna: The Prophetess (Luke 2:36-38)
Anna was very patient. She believed that she would meet the long-awaited saviour, and she was rewarded as she met Him being taken into the temple. That is what she'd heard God speak to her.

The Daughters Of Zelophehad: Inherited The Tribal Portion (Numbers 27:1-11)
Against the narrative and convention of the day, these five women, all sisters, had no father, brothers, husbands or sons. The local custom, at that time, was for men to be the inheritors of land and

not women. However, these women were bold, and they went to speak with the leaders: Moses and Eleazar, the priest. They went before the princes at the door of the tabernacle. Moses asked God what should be done *(shame he didn't do that before it came to this)* and God said, these daughters speak rightly, they are due to inherit - the inheritance of their father! Not only them, but God also said this should now be the custom; women could inherit from their father, if there was no son. If there were no children at all, then the inheritance went to his brothers.

Deborah: The Prophetess And Judge/Warrior (Judges 4)

She took the lead when the men were all moaning to God about the opposing army. Take note here, she was a woman who was already a judge and a prophetess! So much for patriarchal– huh? Deborah approached Barak and suggested a plan of attack, and his reply was he wouldn't do it unless she went with him. *(I guess he perhaps didn't trust her. So, to demonstrate she believed the plan would be successful, she accompanied him but stated that the honour of the won battle would pass to her, as she would also vanquish the opposing leader).* Deborah was bold, and brave and knew the art of war.

Mary: Mother of Jesus (Luke 1:28-30)

Mary was HIGHLY favoured because she believed what Gabriel said would come to pass, despite the horrid social situation, it would plummet her into! She gave birth to and reared the saviour of the world!

Samuel: Went to a Widow at Zarephath (1 Kings 17:7-16)

It was a widow that put a roof over the head of this prophet. The very prophet who was to anoint the first king of the nation of Israel! Yes, a woman with a young child, living on her own, took in a man who was on his own. Due to this, she and her son both survived the famine. Surviving a famine sure looks like favour to me! I believe custom has it that she was also able to provide for neighbours!

Jesus: Meeting A Woman Of Ill Repute (John 4:6)

This woman was not ignored by Jesus— far from it! He purposefully engaged in conversation, drawing her in with His apparent demands for water! Not only was she a woman, but a "dirty" Samaritan! They had a huge conversation before He revealed that He was the messiah they had been waiting for! She then ran back to the village and got all the men therein to come and see for themselves, which they did. It seems strange that if they were a society that treated women as unworthy, these men not only listened to her but then took action! The whole town made their way to the area of the well, and for two days, Jesus told them about the Kingdom! All on the word of a scarlet woman! *Hmmm*, it sure looks like God favouring a woman to me. Jesus could have gone into the town himself, or the disciples could have told people about Him, but there is no mention of that. So the Lord favoured this woman over the men of the town and His disciples!

There are hundreds of women mentioned in the Bible, and also other contemporary non-canonised accounts *(canonization is the process by which the books of the Bible were designated as authoritative)*, documents and writings such as the Septuagint, Catholic Bible, and Apocrypha *(the early church fathers chose not to include certain accounts whilst favouring others)*. A lot of books within the Bible actually reference non-canonised writings! That's what the Bible is, a collection of books, manuscripts, scrolls, and parchment fragments. Again, if you are wanting to find out the truth in that statement, type into a search engine, "non-canonical books referenced in the Bible." There are also deuterocanonical books, which means belonging to the second canon.

I would advise caution when checking this out to not get too attracted to looking up further sources or even purchasing copies of these writings; lest you be led down a fruitless bunny trail. If you are going to be producing a specific work, podcast or even book of your own it is beneficial to know your sources and the sources to which the biblical writers referred. Our mandate is clear, to let people know about the Kingdom of God; that it's at hand and how by accepting Jesus's blood-bought sacrifice others can access its treasures.

These acknowledged women of God were often women of authority, with equal rights, who could rule, challenge leaders, challenge men, be listened to by men when judging, speaking, and prophesying, make decisions, have legal rights, run a business or trade, and take up arms! They were prophets, queens, soldiers, warriors, and judges! The passages which show women as subjugated do not showcase that God saw women as unequal any more than it showcases men as ruling over them and being dictated to or directed by God. Religious rituals were created and adapted according to the social climate of the time; you know what Jesus thought of religion don't you? Over the centuries, both pre-written and documented evidence does not indicate that God chose a patriarchal society, but rather chose, like us in modern Western culture, diversity. Yes, there are instances where God has called for a male leadership structure, but as you read through some of the accounts of those times, there are women amongst it. So perhaps there was no gender intended when the words interpreted as "man" were written. Perhaps it meant person/people as in mankind, not man/male, much like nowadays with all of this gender stuff. We shouldn't have different titles for male or female job roles and titles. It was certain cultures and religions that separated women out.

God's Favoured Women

In ancient cultures, men cooked and women were shepherds. In those cultures, the wife could tell her husband to take a concubine or slave into the bed chamber to beget children. It was men who chose to have shrine prostitutes, not God. When God made the human race, he chose two to start a family where there would be godly offspring. Later, when the tragic murder of one of their sons confirms, mankind, even God's chosen family, had developed fatal flaws; the root of which was Adam and Eve choosing another master. A flaw that had subverted creation everywhere except Eden. Ultimately, the enemy got God's two finest specimens and corrupted them with the touch of death, their destiny and captivity were death. It wasn't until Jesus came into the earth's realm, that death, sin, sickness, and captivity were reversed for all of mankind. Why do I say this? You need to know just how much God loves you! He freed you from the bondage of death and from captivity.

Perhaps we need to reaffirm our identity. It is only when we know our identity that the world at large will begin to understand theirs. In these times in which we are living, identity seems to be unclassified, unknown, or simply ignored. In my opinion, and I don't think I'm alone in this, the veil needs to come off of the eyes of believers! We need a thorough understanding of the scriptures, the variations within scripture, and to question why the Word of God has become so divisive and misunderstood; representing God as an ogre even. Who wants Him as a Father, right? If we don't recognise our identity, then we are orphans. Children who don't know their father often have trouble with their identity. This was a problem I had, and it has taken me twenty-five born-again years to recognise and deal with it!

Before you read any further, do look up these accounts of God favouring women. Just type into a search engine:

- Powerful women of God.
- Who are the women God spoke to in the Bible?
- Which women did Jesus speak to in the Bible?

In studying the scriptures for the account of Abigail, who is one of my top ten heroines of the Bible, I found more pearls of knowledge by just studying the verses I've quoted! I would thoroughly recommend researching for future studies; especially if you decide to decipher some scriptures you feel have been misquoted. Then, you can go back to a translation that includes a Strongs Concordance. Going back to the original languages can reveal so much. I use the *Blue Letter Bible* online (there's also an app version for smartphones). I know the King James Version and the NASB has the Strongs Concordance. I believe the NASB is a more straightforward language!

Perhaps I'll write a book on my favourite favoured women of God one day in the not-too-distant future!

"Strong women don't have attitudes, we have standards." – Marilyn Munroe

"I am not free while any woman is unfree, even when her shackles are very different from my own." – Audrey Lorde

PRAYER

Father God, thank you that there is no gender required in Heaven! That once we are saved, we are no longer categorised the way "man" categorises. We are given a new identity, and You even say that we will be given a new name *(Revelation 2:17)*. I am Your son which also means daughter, by adoption. My father is the rider of the clouds and You provide, heal, and love unconditionally those who are Yours! Sorry that I've sometimes acted and behaved like an orphan; please forgive me. My circumstances don't determine the quantity or quality of love You have for me. I have been given free will, same as the person who is treating me in a way that does not show love, respect, and equality. You will not overwrite anyone's free will. Humans still make terrible mistakes, decisions, and messes; even those whom You've adopted. I ask that You correct me where needed and leave it to You to do as You will with a persecutor. It is not my job to mete out justice, but it is Yours. It is not up to me to seek revenge, because You will avenge me. Thank you that You give me grace and strength as I lean into Your presence. Please help me to be like Your ladies of the Bible, resilient, interdependent, and guided by You. Raise up Your sons & daughters to proclaim the Kingdom of Heaven is at hand; it's within reach! Help me to strengthen the weak, feed the hungry, release captives and love people the way You do.

In Jesus, Yeshua Ha Mashiac's name. AMEN

Chapter Eighteen

Forgiveness

"Beloved, don't be obsessed with taking revenge, but leave that to God's righteous justice, for the scriptures say: If you don't take justice in your own hands, I will release justice for you says the Lord" (Romans 12:19, TPT)

Romans 12:20-21 tells us if your enemy is hungry, buy him lunch—yes, done that one! Win him over with your kindness. Your generosity will awaken his conscience, and God will reward you with favour. Never let evil defeat you, but defeat evil with good. Sound advice from this letter to the Romans. We can never fight evil with evil; because that is a house divided, meaning you are in the same house, kingdom, or boat. We must fight evil from heaven's perspective. After all, you are a Kingdom citizen and the Kings' very own offspring!

So often we remember this when it comes to what we say to others, and I don't know about you, but I have been guilty of speaking bad words over myself.

This is something that you will have heard countless times—forgive and live! Forgiveness is key to your freedom, beloved. Not least you will probably need to forgive yourself, and not only once. We see through a glass darkly, think of it as putting on glasses or sunglasses that are smeared with fingerprints. We sometimes can't help it when we can't see things in focus and when you have had a season of busyness, you can't see the wood for the trees! Hindsight is a wonderful gift, but it only comes after a situation.

I hear you say, *but surely we should have seen these things as they were happening.* No, you couldn't see it because you were so busy either trying to make it stop or by being busy with things that make your heart sing—if that was also possible!

I'm sure you've heard this too; forgiveness doesn't mean it is wiped from your memory. Forgiveness doesn't mean the oppressor gets access to your life. Moving out and moving away doesn't indicate unforgiveness. Talking about your experiences is all about processing the pain and internal conflict. Forgiving someone doesn't presuppose you are going to restore the relationship. Marriage is not something to be worshipped. It is a union between two consenting people in agreement. The two individuals are more important than the union; both people need help, forgiveness, and freedom from bondage. The worst of this statement is that it often takes ages for one to realise the bondage they are in. By then a persecutor is so far down this errant route that he has convinced himself he is a victim of the other, or conversely will be in complete denial of any wrongdoing, using scriptures to back them and subterfuge to brush over and avoid answering anything like a direct question.

FORGIVING MISGUIDED HELP

"Watch over your heart with all diligence, for from it flow the springs of life"
(Proverbs 4:23 NASB).

Forgiveness may also need to be extended to those who have tried to help your marriage. This doesn't mean going to each person whom you've felt has said things which have hurt you or that perhaps caused some inner turmoil. They probably don't even know they've said something that hurt. There is a time to speak and a time to be silent. Well-meaning friends cannot be expected, to respond appropriately, especially those who may be carrying their own unhealed wounds. People who have offered advice and sometimes veiled judgement were trying to support you as best they

Forgiveness

can. Sometimes it can be a momentary lapse of understanding on their part, a misguided attempt at tough talk such as, *come on, put your big girl pants on* or *well there are two sides and you played your part in it.* There are many things that have been said to me, and even as I write, there is still misunderstanding on their part as to the real reasons I ended up initiating divorce proceedings. I simply hadn't expressed clearly enough, nor did I feel able to at the time. We can't go around giving the full disclosure of events to people, especially those who fall on the side of your spouse because surely it will fall on deaf ears! Your spouse will undoubtedly believe you to have pulled the rug out from under his feet: no doubt acting the victim and going around looking beat up and rejected. Don't even spend time thinking about it. Humans are so complex, and it's not your job to make it right for them. Enough injustice has probably occurred already. If you go through divorce procedures his true colours will surface.

Forgiveness is a little bit like dying to self, don't you think? It seems counter to everything that screams for immediate justice. It's not wrong to seek justice, not wrong at all. But true forgiveness is about letting go of that person's possible payment for their sin and allowing God to be the judge. When a person dies, they are no more. Having recently lost my son and visiting his grave, I realised the true meaning of death. It finally sunk in. A dead man is no longer in a position to do anything about what has been done or not done. So to be a "dead" person, yet still forgive is a privilege.

In the word of God, it says we have died to our old life and are now a temple of the Holy Spirit. It is no longer I who lives, but Christ in me, the hope of glory. We are dead. Our body is not ours, but instead, it is inhabited by the living word! We are a holy habitation! What I'm saying here is that scripture can be misunderstood. It doesn't mean letting those who profess to love us be spiteful, harmful and abuse us. In the New Testament, even slave owners were encouraged to be kind to their slaves. In Jeremiah 34, slaves were to be set free after six years!

If we are therefore dead, and we are now in Christ, the abuser/user/oppressor is doing it to Christ. Another scripture says to do everything as unto the Lord. I appreciate that is to do with work, but surely all things in all areas should be as worship. So we do marriage, and divorce as unto the Lord with humility. The King will answer and say to them, "Truly I say to you, to the extent that you did it for one of the least of these brothers or sisters of Mine, you did it for Me" Matthew 25:40, NASB.

It's highly challenging to forgive someone who hates you–I know. It's especially hard when it's someone who promised to love you. Someone who expressed from day one that they loved you so much they wanted to spend the rest of their days with you. Yes, I said HATE! They're not loving you if they are being angry, hateful, disrespectful, uncaring, physically hurting you, or sexually violating you. That beloved is called abuse; the Bible calls it oppression. "Everyone who hates his brother is a murderer, and you know that no murderer has eternal life abiding in him" (1 John 3:15, NASB)

Be at Peace

"Death and life are in the power of the tongue" (Proverbs 4:23, NASB).

Hold back when you feel yourself about to speak badly of your spouse. The anger will escalate, and you probably won't sleep well later. A husband in bondage to the enemy, and by behaviour rejecting the headship of God has put himself in bed with the enemy–sometimes literally! He is mistreating his wife and therefore hating his own body because the two are one flesh. By putting his body through anguish, he is separating himself and covering his garment with violence:

Forgiveness

Husbands love your wives, just as Christ also loved the church and gave Himself up for her, so that He might sanctify her, having cleansed her by the washing of water with the word, that He might present to Himself the church in all her glory, having no spot or wrinkle or any such thing; but that she would be holy and blameless. So husbands also ought to love their own wives as their own bodies. He who loves his own wife loves himself; for no one ever hated his own flesh, but nourishes and cherishes it, just as Christ also does the church, because we are parts of His body. **FOR THIS REASON, A MAN SHALL LEAVE HIS FATHER AND HIS MOTHER AND BE JOINED TO HIS WIFE, AND THE TWO SHALL BECOME ONE FLESH.** *This mystery is great, but I am speaking with reference to Christ and the church. Nevertheless, as for you individually, each husband is to love his own wife the same as himself, and the wife must see to it that she respects her husband.*
Ephesians 5:25-33 BLB Berean Literal Bible

By his actions, he is a slave orphaned by not honouring his father: in bondage and engaging in spiritual adultery. He is worse than a gentile (unbeliever). Completely cut off from the covering of God. You are now unevenly yoked with an unbeliever. Before that, you were unevenly yoked with a man confessing to be a believer but behaving like an orphan. An orphan doesn't believe God loves them. The converse of that is that he can errantly believe that he can get away with murder because God will not judge him but will forgive him.

The root of abuse is hatred, which in turn is the biblical equivalence of murder. Divorce does not end an abusive relationship; the betrayal of trust (treachery), which is treason against the Kingdom of God ends the relationship. Treason, whether the treason of adultery or the treason of hateful treachery, departs the marriage covenant which was made between God, you, and the husband. Treason refers to the betrayal of one's own country, in this case, God's Kingdom; the King's domain, by attempting to overthrow the government (by overthrowing Jesus who governs over us) through waging war against the state or materially aiding its enemies who are Satan, the Anti-Christ, fallen angels and demons.

In a post from Patrick Weaver on his Facebook community which supports abuse victims (and he also heads up a charity called The Exodus Project), he writes, "The demonic embrace of hate by an abuser not only commits spiritual adultery against God, it commits marital treason. The root of abuse is hatred." He goes on to say, "The bible clearly states, no husband sent by God can hate his wife because hate is equivalent to murder, and murder, (mentally, emotionally or physically) is a demonic mentality that co-operates with the forces of darkness to put God's child into bondage and bring about their demise through treacherous behaviour." Now I know this sounds pretty extreme but having seen a demon take possession of my husband, during extreme abuse sessions, I frankly agree with this statement.

Firstly, in the context of marital abuse, the abuser has already broken the marriage covenant. He's left the marriage, even if he is physically still under the same roof. Therefore, the legal divorcing bit is purely a legal duty. Think of it as a get-out-of-jail-free card (only usually there is a high cost)!

It might be useful to remember that the person who has wronged you has also wronged God, and it is up to them to sort that out—not you. If God forgives that person then we should forgive that person. It's not for us to second guess if that person is or isn't repentant. Sorry is often used as a platitude after being challenged or caught and can be in the absence of genuine sorrow; this is usually evidenced by a change in their behaviour. However, the change may only be a temporary show! We no longer need to feel attached to that person, we're no longer one, but two distinct people. Let God be God.

Forgiveness

Still, it remains our privilege to take the moral high ground and forgive a person. Sometimes you may have to do it over and over again. I, for sure, utilised this option! Until the last time you do it and suddenly, you realise that you haven't had a thought about the offender in a while. It's like they have left your inner world; that is because they have! You aren't dragging them around with you anymore! No thoughts of "I hope they have their comeuppance!"

Divorce is and has been such an issue over the centuries, both in the secular world and the church world. Right up until the present time in the church world, it is still a hugely debated topic. I don't really know why the church has always seemed to focus on sexual immorality and then divorce as the main or most contended sins. In the area of sexual immorality, they seem to have forgotten the word of God; but with divorce, well that has caused such division. That is not your problem to solve, nor your primary battle. Once you have recovered and recentered on Christ, you may be able to join the ever-expanding ranks of healed hearts who take up the baton of educating the body of Christ. First, you will need to return to your first love who is Christ. Let Him win back your heart. A wounded heart creates blind spots! You may find you need to forgive the church, both your church, small c, and the Church as a whole, big C.

As I've been writing this, it has helped me to see that within these pages, yet more questions need to be asked: more scriptures, clarifications, and solutions sought. The issue of domination, manipulation, and control is as complex as the humans who embrace it and are victims of it. It could even be suggested that perpetrators are victims too. At the very least, I can guarantee many perpetrators perceive themselves to be victims of desertion, unforgiveness, and false accusation.

God has given all human beings free will. If your husband has decided that what he's doing doesn't need to stop or isn't a problem, then it's up to you to remove yourself from the problem. What is of primary importance is for you to know deep inside that God has not deserted you. You aren't a second-class citizen of heaven, there are no second-class citizens. You are a child of God, a citizen of Heaven, and a bond-servant of God. He does not treat His servants badly, because they are His children. Our lives are supposed to radiate God's love. It's not what we do alone, but it's also who we are, and more importantly whose we are. You cannot serve two masters–choose God.

It's no good for us trying to tell the world there is a problem. They already know. We don't seem to be very good at telling the church there is a problem. The church doesn't seem to think it happens. God has given us free will because He loves us. If your husband is not Christ-like, it's time to put a boundary in place.

> "Never forget the three powerful resources you always have available to you: love, prayer, and forgiveness."
> – H. Jackson Brown, Jr., *Life's Little Instruction Book*

PRAYER:

Lord God, I come before You stripped of any agenda. I humbly bow before You and ask for forgiveness for my hardness of heart formed from the callouses of life. Thank you, Lord, that You assure us that when we forgive others, we will be forgiven. It also demonstrates how much we understand Your forgiveness of us. I know You love me with an everlasting love, which nothing in heaven or on earth can separate me from. Help me to release those who have not honoured me, protected me, and loved me the way they were supposed to. I release *(insert name here)* (and repeat until nothing else comes) from any bad intent, words, curses, and actions I may have taken. I recant those words and turn away from perpetuating sin by taking action that is Yours to take.

Forgiveness

Please be my justice, I seek Your justice Lord, and Your peace as I wait on You. You are my reason to wake up in the morning. I embrace life from this moment on. Life in abundance. Please help me to love like You do, help me to trust again.

In Jesus, Yeshua Ha Mashiac's name. AMEN

Chapter Nineteen

More Than A Conqueror

"In all things we are more than conquerors through Him that loved us"
(Romans 8:37 WBT)

As we wrap up this exercise in fully understanding the problem, the word of God, and the part we play, it would be good to review the journey we've taken.

In the first chapters, we saw the statistics for abuse within Christian marriages are inordinately greater than in the world and I shared my personal story. Our individual journeys are all different, with unique sets of circumstances. I don't want you to compare what you are feeling and experiencing in your marriage to mine, or anybody else's. If something is harming you, it's harming you. Just because it is or is not physical doesn't render it any more or less harmful.

My desire is to see this travesty acknowledged openly within the church, and in order for that to happen women are going to need to be brave. Are you going to be brave? For your sake? If so much is resting on you, you owe it to yourself to be healed, because that will lead you into the deeper love of God. If this injustice stays in the dark what will our Saviour find when He returns? The love of many has grown cold.

We found out from the Bible, our true identity, is not merely as "helpers," but as equal partners in the communion of marriage. How the church is in fact acknowledging some pockets of sinfulness, and yet the figures for abuse, as yet unrecognised, speak for themselves! We are warriors, royalty, and children of God, and He loves us so much; of course, though God does hate divorce, it's not a sin to divorce. Divorce doesn't end the marriage. God hates men who use violence, including through words, remembering abuse is oppression, and oppression is akin to showing contempt towards God. He will not hear their prayers, and He will not override another person's free will to answer ours in the way we want.

> *Just because it is or is not physical doesn't render it any more or less harmful.*

The different types of abuse from very subtle to overt aggression were all exposed. Although there are no doubt many other creative ways to gain control over other people, in particular, spiritual abuse which is unique to church culture; all are serious, and cause visible and invisible wounds.

I trust that the word of God within this book has convinced you that God loves you and that He is for you, not against you. I would love to know how you get on with further study of God's word in several different versions in order to get a balanced overview of what God is saying to His humans, as well as what He's not saying! Women and men, through the blood of Jesus, are equal! We are to submit to one another! Perhaps one day, women will not shudder when they hear the word "submit." The letter of the law kills, but the Spirit brings life.

> "Such confidence we have through Christ before God. Not that we are competent in ourselves to claim anything for ourselves, but our competence comes from God. He has made us competent as ministers of a new covenant—not of the letter but of the Spirit; for the letter kills, but the Spirit gives life" (2 Corinthians 3:4-6, NIV).

Finally, I have included a list of signs of possible abuse, and also the reasons why many women stay silent. That we do and have done for so long is heartbreaking. We looked at some psychological profiling with the triangles to give clarity during "debates!" Purposely, I followed on with some women in the Bible who broke the mould, heroes of ours, yet pretty much ordinary wives. They just had an ear towards God Almighty.

Beloved, you are the apple of God's eye, and the Bride of Christ. He has loved you with everlasting love.rgiveness is the key to enjoying freedom, but first, you must come away from the toxic unequal relationship that has drawn you to reading this (Unless you're reading this for a friend).

You are on your way to freedom.
You have the keys to your new life—fly!

I leave you with this quote from Rosa Parks, an American activist in the Civil Rights Movement, (also known as, the First Lady of Civil Rights), who as a young child witnessed the Ku Klux Klan burning negro churches and schools as well as flogging and killing negros, as they hid inside their home whilst grandpa guarded with rifle in hand. She said, "I have learned over the years that when one's mind is made up, this diminishes the fear; knowing what must be done does away with fear!"

Another is Emmeline Pankhurst, leader of the Suffragette Movement and political activist, "Men make the moral code and they expect women to accept it. They have decided that it is entirely right and proper for men to fight for their liberties and their rights, but that it is not right and proper for women to fight for theirs."

> "The LORD appeared to us in the past, saying: 'I have loved you with an everlasting love; therefore I have drawn you with loving devotion. Again I will build you, and you will be rebuilt, O Virgin Israel. Again you will take up your tambourines and go out in joyful dancing." Jeremiah 31:3-4.

MY PRAYER FOR YOU: A BLESSING

May God our everlasting Father, King of Kings, woo you to His breast, singing songs of delight over you. May His tears be a salve to your wounds. May His sword of truth surgically remove the calluses and scars. May you know that your tears have been collected by His servants, the angels. May you once more rejoice in your complete salvation, the *sozo* that brings healing and peace to your spirit, body, and soul. You are His BRIDE. You are His BELOVED. He's calling you out into the open spaces and wants to dance with you. Let Him lead you beloved, let Him lead.

In Jesus, Yeshua Ha Mashiac's name. AMEN

Contact The Author

lifewithoutlimits1926.co.uk

daisychainsforcrowns.org

YouTube: Eeek...let's talk@Eeek923 (we go where others won't)

Twitter: @EeekElizabeth

Facebook: Elizabeth Kirsten

Facebook support group- Daisy Chains group is secret / private for confidentiality. For information or invitation to join, message Elizabeth Kirsten through Facebook, Whatsapp or Email

Email: lifewithoutlimits1926@gmail.com
WhatsApp: +44 7787 522339
https://whatsapp.com/dl/

Socials: fb:Elizabeth Kirsten
https://www.facebook.com/beth.christian.3910

Other Books:
God Belongs in Business – Collaboration/ Co- Author

Bibliography

Baskerville, G. *"Adultery, Abuse, Abandonment Are Biblical Grounds for Divorce." Life-Saving Divorce.* https://lifesavingdivorce.com/

Choice, Eloise, *Eve or Evolution?* (November 10, 2016). Dialogo Journal, Vol. 3, No. 1, 2016, Available at SSRN: https://ssrn.com/abstract=3059871

Gray, John. *Men are from Mars: Women are from Venus: A Practical Guide For Improving Communication And Getting What You Want In Your Relationships.* New York, NY, HarperCollins Publishers, 1992.

Hart, Lucinda van der. "Domestic Violence and the UK Church." *Premier Christianity*, (20 Dec. 2013). www.premierchristianity.com/home/domestic-violence-and-the-uk-church/711.article.

Hodal, Kate. "One in 200 People Is a Slave. Why?" *The Guardian*, Guardian News and Media, 25 Feb.2019, https://www.theguardian.com/news/2019/feb/25/modern-slavery-trafficking-persons-one-in-200.

Home Office Statistical bulletin - *ASU Center for Problem-Oriented Policing*, 2005. https://popcenter.asu.edu/sites/default/files/problems/bicycle_theft/PDFs/Nicholas_etal_2005.pdf

Hooks, Bell. *All about Love: New Visions*. William Morrow, an Imprint of HarperCollins Publishers, 2022.

Keys of the Kingdom Holy Bible: A New Organic Restoration of The. (2022). Filament Publishing Ltd.

Lane, Erin. "Feminine Wiles - When and When Not to Use Them." *Independent Femme.* 13 Apr. 2021 https://independentfemme.com/feminine-wiles-what-are-they.

Lisitsa, "The Four Horsemen: Contempt." *The Gottman Institute.* https://www.Gottman.com. 9 May 2022 www.gottman.com/blog/the-four-horsemen-contempt/.

Pitzer, Danielle. "Sexual Assault and Rape: Help for Teens." *Focus on the Family*, 4 Apr. 2022. www.focusonthefamily.com/parenting/sexual-assault-and-rape-help-for-teens/. Accessed 02 June 2023.

Strickland, Darby A. Is It Abuse? A Biblical Guide to Identifying Domestic Abuse and Helping Victims. P&R Publishing, 2020.

Thayer, Joseph H. *Thayer's Greek English Lexicon.* Hendrickson Publishers, 2007.

References

https://www.lwa.org.uk/understanding-abuse/statistics

https://www.rapecrisis.org.uk/get-informed/statistic

www.puzzlepiecelaw.co.uk/domestic-abuse

https://www.England.shelter.org.uk

https://ifstudies.org/

https://www.unseenuk.org/

https://lifesavingdivorce.com/

https://theweek.com/

https://www.churchofengland.org/

https://christianitytoday.com/

What is Spiritual Abuse?
https://www.christianitytoday.com/scot-mcknight/2020/december/what-is-spiritual-abuse-working-definition.html

https://www.nacr.org/nacr-institute/pastoral-care-and-abuse/spiritual-abuse

https://www.workthegreymatter.com/bible-marital-rape-jesus-divorce/

Printed in Great Britain
by Amazon